The Debt Pit Escape Plan

Get Creditors Off Your Back, Climb Out of Debt and Rebuild Your Credit

Keoni Gordon

© **Copyright 2020 - All rights reserved.**

The content contained within this book may not be reproduced, duplicated or transmitted without direct written permission from the author or the publisher.

Under no circumstances will any blame or legal responsibility be held against the publisher, or author, for any damages, reparation, or monetary loss due to the information contained within this book, either directly or indirectly.

Legal Notice:

This book is copyright protected. It is only for personal use. You cannot amend, distribute, sell, use, quote or paraphrase any part, or the content within this book, without the consent of the author or publisher.

Disclaimer Notice:

Please note the information contained within this document is for educational and entertainment purposes only. All effort has been executed to present accurate, up to date, reliable, complete information. No warranties of any kind are declared or implied. Readers acknowledge that the author is not engaged in the rendering of legal, financial, medical or professional advice. The content within this book has been derived from various sources. Please consult a licensed professional before attempting any techniques outlined in this book.

By reading this document, the reader agrees that under no circumstances is the author responsible for any losses, direct or indirect, that are incurred as a result of the use of the information contained within this document, including, but not limited to, errors, omissions, or inaccuracies.

Table of Contents

INTRODUCTION 1

    YOU ARE NOT ALONE 2
    SIMILAR STORIES 4

CHAPTER 1: IN THE HOLE 7

    FINANCIAL ASSESSMENT 8
    PERSONAL RESPONSIBILITY 12
    THERE IS A WAY OUT 15
    MOTIVATION THROUGH TOUGH TIMES 23

CHAPTER 2: THE DEBT PIT TRAP 29

    REASONS WHY PEOPLE GO INTO DEBT 30
    WHY DO PEOPLE CHOOSE TO STAY IN DEBT? 41
    DEBT PIT TRAP DESIGN 45
    THE CREDIT CARD REVOLUTION 47

CHAPTER 3: STOP DIGGING 51

    BECOME INFORMED 52
    CATCH UP DEFAULT ACCOUNTS 53
    CUT UP ALL YOUR CREDIT CARDS 53
    MINIMIZE LIVING EXPENSES 54
    BUILDING A BUDGET 54
    SETTING UP A BUDGET 56
        Step 1: Know Why You Want a Budget 56
        Step 2: Income and Expenses 58
        Final Step: Reviewing Your Expenses 63
    SET UP A SAVINGS ACCOUNT 64
    SET UP PAYMENT PLANS 65
    OTHER SOLUTIONS 66

CHAPTER 4: DEALING WITH CREDITORS 69

GET CREDITORS OFF YOUR BACK WITHOUT LOSING YOUR SHIRT	69
SELLING OF DEFAULT DEBT	70
LAST-DITCH ATTEMPTS BY CREDITORS	71
LEGAL ADVICE	76
UNDERSTANDING DEBT COLLECTORS	80

CHAPTER 5: CLIMB OUT 83

CUT COSTS THROUGH FRUGAL LIVING	86
QUICKER WAYS TO GET OUT OF DEBT	94
COMMON MISTAKES	101
WHAT'S YOUR MOTIVATION?	104

CHAPTER 6: REBUILD YOUR CREDIT 109

HOW TO REBUILD YOUR CREDIT	110
STEP 1: OBTAIN A COPY OF YOUR CREDIT SCORE	110
STEP 2: PAY ON TIME ALL THE TIME	111
STEP 3: WORKING WITH CREDIT CARDS	112
STEP 4: REBUILDING YOUR CREDIT SCORE	114
STEP 5: CHANGE CREDIT BEHAVIOR	115
REBUILDING	118
HOW TO REBUILD CREDIT FAST	119
AFTER BANKRUPTCY	120

CHAPTER 7: STAY OUT 125

HOW TO STAY OUT OF DEBT	126
GOOD MONEY HABITS	147

CONCLUSION 153

DEBT-FREE LIVING	153
HOW TO LIVE A DEBT-FREE LIFE	162
MAINTAIN A DEBT-FREE LIFESTYLE	167
WHAT A DEBT-FREE LIFESTYLE REALLY LOOKS LIKE	170

REFERENCES 179

IMAGE REFERENCES 187

Introduction

Let's face it—they didn't do a good job teaching us about personal finance in school.

Sure, some people took accounting courses or may have been taught good money habits from their parents. But what if you were like me and didn't learn anything about how to manage money until it was too late, and you were drowning in debt?

I was like that a couple of years ago. Every time my phone rang, I used to cringe, especially whenever the caller ID indicated it was yet another collection agency. Eventually, it felt as though I had more "blocked numbers" on my phone than normal contacts, and I got tired of letting the calls just ring or shutting my phone off. I felt completely helpless and my situation felt completely hopeless, as a mountain of debt seemed to pile up around me, no matter how hard I tried to dig myself out from under it.

Financially, things seemed to go from bad to worse. Of course, focusing on it constantly only added to my frustration. I felt like a failure; I felt that I had not only failed myself in not being able to be financially self-sufficient, but I had failed my family by not being able to provide a decent lifestyle for them. Despite feelings of failure, I also felt completely isolated and alone in this debt trap.

Well, I'm here to tell you that you are definitely not alone. I should know, given my own experience. I have also shared stories with people from all walks of life across the US who have found themselves in similar situations.

You Are Not Alone

It's time to take heart and realize there are more Americans in debt than you could possibly imagine. Most bad debt comes from several places, though it is often a result of overdue balances. The first of these are overdue medical expenses. These costs have usually been incurred as a shortfall between what medical insurance is prepared to pay and the total balance. A whopping 20% of American households are facing debt collectors thanks to unpaid medical costs.

It's estimated that almost 33% of all Americans have debt that has been handed over to a collection agency. This debt ranges from around $1,450 to extensive student loans that are tens of thousands of dollars. The average student loan can range from $30,000 to $90,000. For most young graduates, repaying this debt is impossible, and many live frugally, working two to three jobs seven days per week to crawl out of the hole. This debt is even more difficult to pay off when the unemployment rate is currently so high.

While trying to build up a credit rating, they fall into the trap of taking on credit cards and use these to supplement their income. Unfortunately, this is robbing Peter to pay Paul, and they soon discover that they are now simply adding to a mountain of debt, with truly little to show for it.

Problems that accompany mounting debt include all those negative thoughts that make you focus on "lack and what you don't have". The Ascent surveyed 1,007 people who had varying degrees of debt. They discovered that 78% of those with debt think about it at least once a day. Naturally, this will have a negative impact on productivity and anything else you're meant to be doing. How can you be fully focused on anything if your mind is wandering elsewhere?

Problems associated with debt can't always be measured financially. Many of these issues affect all areas of our lives, emotionally, physically, and psychologically. They can negatively influence our relationships with others and even our own thought processes. When we face financial challenges, we have trouble recognizing anything good in the world, and this is why our situation feels so completely hopeless. This is the debt pit that we're currently inhabiting, and if you feel like the walls keep closing in around you, your emotional state is being controlled by this sense of helplessness and hopelessness.

Fear and shame are two other emotions closely attached to debt, owing people money, and not being able to meet your financial obligations. Perhaps you fear that you are never going to get on top of your finances. You may be concerned about your retirement and whether you will have enough to live with when you do retire. You may be anxious and afraid that you will be evicted from your home or face foreclosure. Following the housing crisis between 2007 and 2010 or recent global disasters, your home may have even depreciated in value.

Similar Stories

At 50, Jennifer was forced to undergo major spinal surgery which was not entirely covered by her medical insurance. To make up for the shortfall, she took on what should have been a short-term loan of $20,000. This would have covered the medical costs and helped with living expenses during the three-month recovery time. Returning to work in January, she found herself without a job. The bank refused to honor the loan insurance agreement and today, although she's been paying whatever she can afford, her current loan stands at close to $48,000.

Dave walked away from debt in excess of $2 million resulting from a real estate development that went bad. He'd poured his heart and soul into the business for six years, working seven days a week. It was easier for him to file for bankruptcy where he could keep his home and vehicle. Dave had no intention of losing his business, especially after all the sweat equity he'd put into it, but it was the best available option at the time.

Julia is only 36. She's currently sitting with debt to the tune of $125,000 thanks to a failed marriage, student loans, outstanding medical bills, legal fees from her divorce, as well as various charges accumulated through being evicted on numerous occasions. She feels ashamed of all the debt and has no idea of how she'll ever be able to repay everyone she owes money to.

Upon receiving an inheritance, Sharon was provided with a substantial line of credit. Although she was still grieving at the time, she admits that she quickly added a further $20,000 to her existing debts. Now, she has managed to reduce her outstanding debt by half, but she still has a long way to go. One of her deepest regrets is wasting money on frivolous spending, especially when she should have been mourning.

Benjamin qualified for a professorship which left him in the hole with about $90,000 in student loans. He really wishes that someone somewhere had taught him about the value of money and the importance of being able to repay loans as they were due so he didn't have to face all this with naivete. As an associate professor now, he's uncertain about how quickly he will be able to repay the amounts he's indebted for.

Chapter 1:
In the Hole

You're in the hole (you know that), but how did you get there? While this may be stating the obvious as you're fully aware of the hole you're currently in, it's important to understand how you got there to begin with. Just like there are various reasons why the individuals in the introduction have found themselves in their current financial situation, it's worthwhile understanding what has brought you to this point in your life.

Financial Assessment

One of the ways to do this is by completing a financial assessment to discover how you are really doing financially. This is a self-evaluation. Take a few moments to answer each of the following questions. Be as open and honest as possible. Nobody will see your answers except for you (unless you specifically want to share what you've learned with someone).

This will give you an indication of how you're doing presently when it comes to managing your money.

Key:

- 5 – constantly

- 4 – normally

- 3 – occasionally

- 2 – rarely

1 – never

Instructions:

Next to each question is a space. Assign a number from the key above to each of the following questions. When you are done, tally your total and check it against the summary section found after the questions. This will give you a clear indication as to how you handle your finances.

Questions:

Managing your finances

All of my financial records are organized, and important documents can be found easily if they are needed. ____

At the end of each month, I have enough money to cover my expenses, including my mortgage/rent. ____

I calculate my net worth annually (assets minus debts). ____

I have a checking account with a financial institution (bank) that I use to pay my bills. Indicate "5" for "Yes" and "1" for "No" ____

I have enough money saved for an unforeseen emergency. ____

I know what tax bracket I fall into. ____

My budget for monthly expenses and savings is written down, and I stick to it. _____

My financial goals are written down with exact dollar amounts needed and a specific date by which to achieve them (e.g., $12,000 for a new car in 36-months). _____

Investing or Saving:

After taxes, my investments and savings are greater than the current rate of inflation. _____

I am always saving for the future. These long-term savings include things like retirement, college funds for my children, a home, trips, vehicles, etc. _____

I have enough money set aside to cover expenses for three months in the event of a disaster. _____

In addition to my pension account, I have a private retirement account that I invest in monthly. Indicate "5" for "Yes" and "1" for "No" _____

My investment portfolio is diverse, and I have savings in more than one type of account. _____

My savings increase in direct proportion to my income. _____

Estate Planning & Insurance:

I have medical insurance and other insurance for large expenses such as disability or unplanned medical expenses. _____

My will is current. Indicate "5" for "Yes" and "1" for "No" _____

Credit:

Less than 20% of my monthly income pays for car payments, credit cards, and student loans. _____

My credit cards are paid in full to avoid unnecessary interest being charged. _____

Shopping:

I control the urge to "impulse buy" and work according to a strict purchasing plan when shopping for smaller items. _____

When shopping I compare prices, especially for large ticket purchases. This comparison is done with at least three different sources. _____

Scorecard:

Add each of your totals, and check your scorecard below for the results and possible solutions.

81-100 Your finances are in excellent condition. Be sure to continue with the financial habits you have in place.

61-80 The way you manage your finances is above average. You're doing a great job!

41-60 You're generally moving in the right direction, but you could be doing more.

21-40 If you don't do something to turn your financial management around, you could be heading into financial difficulty. It's not too late to make adjustments where necessary.

0-20 Your current financial situation is unhealthy, and you need help. Don't lose hope, though, because starting today, you can begin to do things to turn this around. It's never too late to begin implementing sound financial habits.

Wherever you scored 1, 2, or 3, consider making changes in these areas first. This will automatically bolster your current finances almost immediately.

Personal Responsibility

Something that we need to make clear right from the very start is that there are only a *few* instances when you can honestly point a finger at others or shrug your shoulders and say that your current debt has become completely out of your control. I'm a firm believer that we each have a choice and can decide for ourselves what course of action we want to take.

An example of when debt is out of one's control is unforeseen medical expenses. Some of the people I spoke with while gathering information for this book have been faced with mountains of debt that are gathering compounding interest each month. Some may have been involved in car accidents that left them in immediate need of extensive medical treatment that is not always covered by medical insurance. It's these unexpected emergency expenses that I can sympathize with.

If, on the other hand, you've accepted credit cards from financial institutions and racked up exorbitant amounts of debt on these, my sympathy begins to wane. You should definitely be mature enough to be able to take full responsibility for this debt. Some of the people I spoke with realized this too late and are often quick to point fingers at the credit card companies for offering them a product that was bound to get them into debt. The very name "credit card" should scream "debt" loud and clear. It's a line of credit that you're being offered. If you enter into a contractual agreement with a bank or financial institution that has offered you a loan, you should be fully aware of all that comes with it.

Of course, there's nothing quite like being able to flash a piece of plastic and get whatever you want immediately, but what about the fine print? Have you read it thoroughly and, more importantly, do you understand it? Are you aware of the ramifications if you cannot repay any of the loan amounts that are attached to your credit card? What is the interest rate that's going to accrue on a monthly basis? Each of these questions needs to be thoroughly answered before you sign on the dotted line.

As is recommended for big-ticket purchases, why not shop around for your best option when it comes to a financial institution? Depending on your credit score, collateral that you may have, and your age, you may find that certain financial institutions offer better package deals. If you're specifically shopping for a credit card, it may pay for you to move your checking account to another financial institution altogether—one where you can benefit from various solutions offered under one umbrella.

Something that should be made clear is this: financial institutions offering lines of credit through credit cards are not predatory or evil! It's not the actual piece of plastic that does the damage when it comes to racking up extensive credit card debt; rather, it's the hands that the credit card is in.

There are too many individuals that are more than happy to shoot down financial institutions for making lines of credit available to individuals from all walks of life. Please understand that nobody is holding a gun to your head and forcing you to accept the credit card or to go on uncontrolled spending sprees with it. There seems to be a complete lack of personal accountability or responsibility when it comes to frivolous spending.

I think that it was only one of the individuals that I interviewed in Chapter 1 who actually owned the fact that they had been irresponsible when it came to their credit card debt. Many others had fallen on hard times and had been living off their credit cards. This is also completely understandable, but I have to raise the question here: if you were either a student or knew that you had a shortfall each month, why make matters worse by signing up for a credit card?

It's important to understand the rules when you decide to sign up for that piece of plastic. The only way to do this is by making sure that you've read and fully understood all the fine print in your credit card contract. I have yet to find one contract that doesn't clearly spell out all of the terms and conditions when it comes to lending. Interest rates are clearly spelled out, as well as what to expect if you default or cannot pay.

Each of these contracts is quite thorough. They have to be because it is a legal contract that you are entering into between yourself and your financial institution. And yes, they do charge an interest rate on your outstanding debt. This is how they make money and keep in business themselves. You cannot hold the bank responsible if you sign the contract, yet you haven't read and understood the fine print.

The same is true of your mortgage. Be certain that you educate yourself about the terms of the agreement. Simply signing something you don't understand because you need the line of credit is absurd. Fast-forward to where you are now. You may be feeling embarrassed or ashamed that you find yourself in this hole where you cannot meet all your financial obligations. While this may be true of your current situation, you've taken the first step toward clawing your way to financial freedom. You will soon begin to feel empowered and ready to take control of your life once more.

There Is a Way Out

The good news is that no matter how great your current debt is, there is a way out. What follows are some amazing examples of individuals, couples, and even families that have been able to carve their way out of some pretty massive debt pits, and many of them have done it in record time.

Dave and Claire

When a simple crisis can bring you to realize that you have a major problem with managing your finances, something has to give. This is the situation that Dave and Claire found themselves in. Both were fortunate enough to have well-paying jobs, but this didn't make them financially savvy. Instead, it had the opposite effect. Things got so bad that they couldn't even afford to buy groceries.

The façade they showed to the rest of the world was one of wealth; they acted as though they were doing well for themselves. In the meantime, they were living from paycheck to paycheck and maxing out their credit cards. The two luxury vehicles, annual exotic holidays, and expensive jewelry screamed to the world that they had money. The truth was that they were about $52,000 in the hole. It finally took their inability to afford food to wake them both up.

A simple spreadsheet assessment allowed them to see exactly where their money was going each month, and this was enough to make them feel physically ill. Neither Dave nor Claire were to blame for their current financial situation—they both were. Their budget showed them that they were spending more than they made. They had no kind of retirement or savings strategy in place (and they wondered why their finances were looking so pear-shaped).

The strategy they used to climb out of their pit of debt was simple:

- They got rid of all their unnecessary "stuff" that they'd accumulated over the years. Within two weeks, they were able to make $2,000 by selling everything they really had no need for on eBay. When they saw this happening, they realized that there was a glimmer of light at the end of the tunnel.

- Next came their credit cards. Between them, they were sitting with ten credit cards (yep, you read that number correctly). It was time to say goodbye to the plastic that they'd use to cushion their expenses for such a long time. Now this is where Dave and Claire actually got it right; instead of just making a decision to no longer use their credit cards, they actually cut each of them up into tiny little pieces, and into the bin they went. These were replaced by two debit cards. The beauty of a debit card is that you cannot spend money that you don't actually have in your account(s).

- They moved on to repaying their MASSIVE outstanding debts by using a debt snowball effect. This is a simple tactic that they learned from a Dave Ramsey podcast. They listed out all of their debt—everything from the smallest outstanding debt to the highest. While paying the minimum amount on each of their debts, the idea was to pay as much as possible toward the smallest debt. If you can imagine it, your debts could all be broken down into four- or five-line items.

- They got rid of their first pile of debt which is usually something that can be done in a month or two. Whatever you would have spent repaying that debt can then be added onto the next one and so on until you manage to pay them all off. Large debts such as high student loans, mortgages, or car repayments can take longer, but working on paying them off is definitely worth getting them off your list.

- Dave and Claire canceled their annual vacations. They literally cut their finances down to the bone. Next came their monthly grocery bill. Rather than shopping wherever they felt such as at boutique-style grocery outlets, they began checking prices at Wal-Mart. This simple change allowed them to cut their grocery bill in half.

There were a couple of additional things that Dave and Claire did to make extra money each month, and every cent of additional income was used to pay off the debt that they owed. Slowly but steadily, they began to see progress, and in just nine months, they were able to pay the final installment that allowed them to be completely debt-free. The main message that they share is that if they can accomplish this in only nine months, anyone can do it.

James and Wendy

James and Wendy met at college and decided to combine their outstanding debt when they married. This soon became overwhelming for them, and the only way out was to file for bankruptcy and try to start again. While this was a short-term solution, James and Wendy soon began accumulating debt once more because their spending habits were never rehabilitated or altered in any way. In addition to this, they still had outstanding student loans, and they were forced to take out car loans once again.

Their debt quickly amassed to almost $200,000.

Here's how James and Wendy managed to settle the above amount in five years:

- When Wendy had their third child, she decided to cash in some of her retirement fund and allocated this toward their debt.

    <u>As a caveat</u>: This is something that's often very tempting when you have retirement funds that you can access. I would not recommend this as a solution. Being able to save for retirement depends on compounding interest that accrued over many years. Reducing these funds in any way

compromises your retirement investment.

- James and Wendy also cut back on vacations and visited with family instead. The cars they replaced for the ones that they lost during bankruptcy were much older, and they drove them for longer (despite what others may have thought of them at the time). Their end goal was to be financially independent and debt-free, and consistently reminding themselves of this goal is what kept them motivated to keep pushing through. Another huge factor was that they realized saving for their future retirement could only really happen once they had managed to get out from under their current debt.

- It took all of five years for James and Wendy to pay off everything that they owed. Now, their only major debt is for a mortgage, which they are trying to pay off more quickly to reduce the amount of interest being charged. This has taught them to budget more carefully and only buy those things that they have the money for. This is also something they are passing on to their children starting at a young age. They are now able to set aside money for college funds for their children, something they were unable to do before.

Dr. Patricia

If you think that debt is only an issue for individuals who are earning middle to low incomes, then the following story will open your eyes as to how even those who are earning very high salaries can rack up incredibly high debt. It has taken Dr. Patricia seven years to decrease her $2 million debt by $1.3 million. So, how does a medical student with a full scholarship end up with such a staggering amount of debt?

Her wake-up call came once she'd submitted her IRS taxes through her financial consultant, expecting to receive funds back. She was completely thrown off guard when her tax return came back stating that she in fact owed the IRS an amount of $16,000. She thought it had to be impossible, and she passed all her financial information on to another financial consultant. They came back with the same response.

Patricia had received a full ride to medical school but decided to opt for a better school instead. While some of her tuition was paid, she was responsible for the $40,000 per year shortfall. Being faced with a large bill from the IRS made Patricia curious as to what else she owed. Sitting down with a spreadsheet, she calculated that her debts tallied just under $2 million dollars. But how did this happen? As a qualified medical practitioner, she was already earning close to six figures a year.

Once she began analyzing where her money was going, she soon discovered that a large portion included outstanding student loans, property, the outstanding amount she owed to the IRS, tuition fees for her children, credit card debts, and other smaller personal loans.

This is how Dr. Patricia began to emerge from her pit of debt:

- For her, it was all about becoming educated and informed about making wise financial decisions. She put a budget together, and instead of living paycheck to paycheck, she started working according to a strict budget. She used the same snowballing loan repayment plan discussed above, and she replaced she and her husband's luxury vehicles with cheaper models that were paid for with cash. Patricia and her husband also decided to refinance their mortgage.

- She cut corners wherever possible and sold their two rental properties; they had already lost money with these properties because they weren't managed properly. For Patricia and her husband, their biggest challenge was delayed gratification. They had lived in such a way that whatever they wanted they would buy and worry about paying it off later. This was a bitter pill for both of them to swallow.

As Patricia was becoming more money conscious and financially-educated, she began speaking to other physicians who she worked with about it. This led to the discovery that she knew more than most, and there were many high-income earners who had absolutely no clue how to manage their money. This led to her starting a Facebook group where physicians could ask finance-related questions in a safe space. She has also since written a book that speaks directly to medical professionals about managing their money better.

Her top three pieces of advice are as follows:

1. Get used to delayed gratification.

2. Learn from those around you who know more than you do.

3. Pay your outstanding accounts aggressively.

Motivation Through Tough Times

Have you ever tried to get out of debt before? Perhaps you wanted to use the money you've been forking out on interest every month, and you're tired of feeling as though you're constantly marking time, or maybe you're tired of the endless phone calls from debt collectors. If you have ever been in a similar situation, you can most likely recall how motivated and enthusiastic you were when you first decided to get out of debt. However, usually, this enthusiasm fades away. So, how can you get your mojo back?

One of the first things that you need to do is review and revise your motivation to change your financial habits. You've already been there before, so there was definitely a reason for wanting to get out of debt. You need to rediscover what this reason was. This can be referred to as your "why". This is what is behind your drive for getting out of debt completely and *staying* out of debt.

Part of this process could be understanding the difference between inspiration and motivation. Jackie Beck is someone who is dedicated to helping others get out of debt after she and her husband managed to pay off over $147,000 of their own debt. According to her, it's only when you understand what your underlying motivation is that you will be able to see it through, even if your repayments are going to take you years to pay off.

Motivation can be permanent if you remain focused on your reason for wanting to get out of debt. Is it to start saving toward retirement or to pay into a college account for your children's tuition fees? Maybe you have your eye on a new car but don't want to get caught up with all the compounding interest, or it's possible that your motivation is simply to be able to sleep peacefully at night without having to worry about all the accounts that are past due or currently sitting in the hands of a collection agency.

Shift your focus to the positive change(s) you expect to occur once you make that final payment and you are finally completely free of outstanding debt. What will your life look like? If you develop a habit and lifestyle change in order to pay your debts, what will you do with the excess funds each month? Think about this, and write all your financial goals down in a journal. These will be all the things that you PLAN to do once you are completely free of outstanding debt. When you're feeling your motivation slipping, turn to these journal entries to remind yourself what you're doing it all for.

Remember, some of the stories we've shared above included people who took several years to pay off some really HUGE debts. If they can do it, then you can definitely work your way out from the pile of debt you have as well. Think about the millions of dollars that Dr. Patricia has managed to pay off to date. You can do this! All you need is to remain focused on the reason you want to be free of the binds that debt puts you in.

There's no such thing as a quick fix when it comes to repaying debt. Some may promise you an easy way out, but please realize that there is no such thing. One of the ways that could potentially assist you is consolidating your debt; however, this will only work if you are disciplined enough to change your spending and financial habits.

It's important to be able to break bad spending habits and replace them with ones that are positive. We don't realize how strong habits can be and how easily they influence our lives, quickly taking over the way we spend our money if we let them. If we are compulsive shoppers or we shop whenever we feel alone or depressed, this could potentially spell disaster for anyone trying to get out of debt. It's our commitment to change that becomes the secret to becoming completely debt-free.

Dream BIG dreams about all the things you plan for your life once you pay off all your debt. Let your imagination run wild (as long as it doesn't involve ordering another credit card!). Dreams of the future are important; they can serve as reminders as to what you're doing this for in the first place. If your dream is to finally own your own home, you can work out how much you need to save for a reasonable down payment.

Shift your mentality from one of instant gratification to one where you are self-sufficient. This may mean delayed gratification, but if there's no debt or compounding interest attached, surely this is a much better option for you. This is truly shown in a study done on children regarding instant gratification.

A group of child psychologists placed a plate in front of some children with two marshmallows on it. The children who were separated but monitored individually were told that if they could resist eating the marshmallows in front of them, they would be rewarded with another two marshmallows. They were to wait between five and ten minutes (depending on the age of the child). It was discovered that there were some children who could manage to wait quite easily, while others simply couldn't resist the temptation directly in front of them, even for the shortest time. These children were followed as they grew into young adults. The same trends occurred. Those who managed the simple marshmallow test became responsible adults who could manage their finances and live within their means, while the others were more prone to spending impulsively.

Being able to persevere in regards to repaying any amount of debt requires daily effort and focus. If you set your mind on doing it, however, you will succeed, and before too long you will enjoy the sweet rewards of getting rid of the noose around your neck that is debt.

Take some time to identify what your main motivators are for getting out of debt. Whenever you feel that you're being drawn back into a financial hole, refer back to this section. Try to identify those times when you feel tempted to overspend. Is there a pattern that presents itself whenever this happens? If so, write this down as well. This will make you more aware of any triggers that could possibly set you off.

The most important takeaway from this section is that there definitely is a way out, and hope exists regardless of how deep in debt you are. It's all up to you to make the decision that you're going to grab hold of the lifeline that's being thrown your way so you can manage to climb out of the debt pit that you're currently in.

Chapter 2:

The Debt Pit Trap

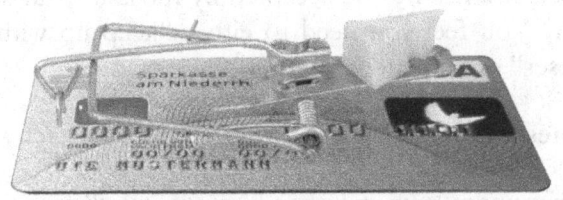

"Bad debt is debt that makes you poorer. I count the mortgage on my home as bad debt, because I'm the one paying on it. Other forms of bad debt are car payments, credit card balances, or other consumer loans." ~ Robert Kiyosaki

Reasons Why People Go Into Debt

Avoiding debt is virtually impossible to do for many reasons which we are going to focus on throughout this chapter. As you work through these reasons there's sure to be some of them that resonate with you.

Acceptance by Others

This debt is usually incurred as a result of peer pressure or out of a need to be accepted by those in your social circle. You feel you need to either "keep up with the Joneses" or be better than they are.

Babies

Welcoming a new member into the family is a really exciting time for most couples, but it comes with a hefty price tag attached. This is especially true if it is a first child or you happen to be expecting twins. Expenses range from rearranging your entire home and decorating nurseries to ensuring that the right car seat has been bought. For young married couples who may be caught unawares, it could even mean replacing a sporty two-seater for something more family-friendly.

Debt doesn't stop when it comes to having the baby; these expenses will now become something that's permanent and increasing on an annual basis as the new addition to the family is going to cost you money until they are old enough to leave home and fend for themselves.

Because We Deserve It

You may have worked hard for an extended period of time and believe that you deserve to reward yourself. This is usually with a large ticket item such as a new car. While this may have felt like a good idea at the time and you had the money to pay the initial down payment, you should realize that you are likely to be tied into a financial contract amounting to the value of the car, as well as all the compounding interest, for approximately a four-year period.

You may have initially felt that you deserved a new car, but once the dust has settled and you think about it realistically, it's possible that you will suffer from buyer's remorse. What makes matters even worse when it comes to cars is that they depreciate in value substantially the second you drive them off the showroom floor or out of the dealer's lot. Even if you decide that you could settle for something more affordable, your chances of being able to recover the full amount is near impossible.

Become Financially Astute

Another major reason for incurring debt is being ignorant when it comes to finances. Nobody is suggesting that you need to become a financial guru, but learning about finances so you can manage your money more effectively is far better than suffering from ostrich syndrome, which is where you believe that if you close your eyes, your problems will all disappear. Naturally, this isn't the case, and if anything, issues become far greater the longer we choose to ignore them.

Business Start-Up Financing

If you've ever decided to start your own business, you know just how quickly money can disappear. One must realize that when they sign for loans to cover their start-up costs, it is not "free money" that they are receiving. Like all loans over a particular term, most of these have the maximum interest added onto the initial capital amount. It's vital that you stick with your minimum payments every month and even try to pay that little extra if you are able. For every additional couple of dollars paid, you could potentially be saving hundreds in compounding interest.

Car Repayments

We've considered the instant gratification side of rushing out to buy a new car, but can you really afford the repayments? Are you prepared should something unforeseen happen (like losing your job)? Car payments are one of the leading causes of debt. When you are paying off a vehicle you got a loan for, try to get the amount owed to zero as quickly as possible to remove a large portion of your debt.

Clothing Accounts

Who doesn't like to dress stylishly and look totally fab? However, the price tag that comes along with any clothing store or retail store account(s) can run up to significant amounts. The problem is that most people are carrying several store credit cards around with them at any given time and rolling the repayments. Once again, this develops the attitude of being able to purchase things on credit now and worrying about paying for them later.

There is seldom any care or thought given when it comes to shopping for clothing or household items, jewelry, or furniture. If you happen to be a compulsive shopper or use shopping as retail therapy to cheer you up, then you need to be extra careful not to max out all your cards simultaneously, making it so you have no way of meeting the minimum payments on each card at the end of the month.

Buying on credit is convenient, and you may even believe that it's a bit of a status symbol being able to haul all the pieces of plastic out of your purse or wallet. However, you need to keep accurate records of where your money is going every month as well as exactly how much you are spending.

Co-Signed Loan Accounts

Be aware when it comes to co-signing any loan documents. Should something happen to the person that you've co-signed for, you are liable for their debt. Ensure that you have read and understood every single clause in the contract so that you don't end up in hot water. Ensure that the person you're co-signing for has the financial means to pay their own debt and that there's sufficient insurance to cover the debt should anything unforeseen happen to them.

Credit Cards

Another major debt generator is credit cards. Several individuals carry almost as many credit cards around with them as they do other retail outlet cards. These get used on fine dining experiences, flights to various states, gasoline, household expenses, and other forms of entertainment. When you consider all of the above, the only expense that you should have is gasoline, and you should only have one card.

Economics

What is happening within your country or throughout the global economy can provide you with a false sense of security. This could be anything from property valuations to low mortgage or interest rates. These things can give you a false sense of security; you might believe that the low rates are going to last. This is often when homeowners take advantage of the situation by taking out loans against their home equity to buy things that they don't really need.

Emergencies

This is another area where debt is often racked up substantially and without warning. Very few individuals have money tucked away for emergencies. Ideally, you should have around three months of income saved for emergencies. So, what constitutes an emergency? Well, this could be anything from major auto repairs to unexpected medical emergencies. In the current economy, it could also come in handy as the unemployment rate is being influenced by COVID-19. Without sufficient savings, times like these can be extremely tough on a household.

Fines

If you have any outstanding traffic fines, these should be paid for as quickly as possible. You should go out of your way to avoid these at all costs as they really are an unnecessary expense.

Funeral Expenses

Wherever possible, take out funeral insurance for your entire family. This will certainly ease an already stressful situation. If you've taken out an insurance policy some time back, be sure that it's still in line with current funeral expenses. Where necessary, either top off your current cover or take out additional cover for you and each member of your immediate family.

Home Renovations

There are certain times when you should avoid home renovations completely, and one of these times is when you're in a financial jam. Unless the renovations are actually vital repairs that you cannot do without, such as leaking or burst pipes, put all major home renovations off until you are able to pay for these in cash.

It's tempting to renovate your home whenever you see one of your neighbors remodeling theirs. However, you aren't aware of their situation. They may have come into some money in the form of an inheritance, or they may be preparing their home to sell. Don't get caught in the middle of neighborhood renovation wars.

Lack of a Budget

Another major cause for getting into unnecessary debt is by spending more than you absolutely need to be spending. This is what happens when you free-spend. An example of free-spending is when you go into the store without a shopping list, and if something looks good, you simply add it to your basket without even looking at the price tag.

When you're working from a budget, you know exactly what is coming into your account(s) each month and what needs to be allocated to outstanding debt; it's knowing exactly what your utilities cost, what your gas budget is, how much money needs to be allocated to credit card debt, your mortgage amount, and so on. Smart choices can be made once getting your finances under control.

Life Choices

As a young adult, some of your life choices such as marriage or being able to afford a home can be delayed because you are still paying off huge student loans. There are various reasons that this happens. Some of these reasons come down to being unable to find suitable employment after graduation. Irrespective of your qualifications, this is a hard fact that many find difficult to swallow. It really seems unfair to have to put your life on hold due to outstanding debt.

Media Influence

Everywhere you look there are media influencers that are paid mega bucks to keep you spending. Everything looks so glamorous on Facebook, Instagram, or on the ads that happen to pop up on the device that you're using to browse the internet. Marketing experts prey on individuals who love shopping. If this is you, then you're likely to be spending money online on a regular basis. There's little you can do to prevent your exposure to all of these advertisements and products flashing before your eyes. This is where having a fixed budget comes in.

Medical Expenses

Even routine medical insurance runs out if you're on chronic medication or require special care for an extended period of time. These costs are usually extremely high and are another major contributor to a large chunk of outstanding debt throughout the US.

Mortgage(s)

This is usually a necessary debt but one that you can pay off fairly quickly if you follow the snowball method of managing your debt. You should have learned from Dr. Patricia in the previous chapter that if you've invested in property to bring in rental income, you should make certain that you are able to cover expenses should your tenants decide to default in payments. Her advice of having a property management organization handle this for you is golden advice.

Needs Versus Wants

Do you genuinely understand the difference between what a need is versus a want? We've become so used to the instant gratification that comes with simply swiping a credit card that the mentality of "no money, no worries; I'll pay for it later" seems to be a common trend. For the individual who deals with depression or anxiety by shopping, the delayed payment is likely to result in even greater anxiety and depression once the credit card statement arrives. This can easily spiral into a vicious cycle.

Outstanding Taxes

Be certain that you're up-to-date on all of your outstanding taxes. The IRS can be completely unforgiving when you owe them money. If you do indeed owe a debt to them and you cannot afford to pay the full amount, contact them to sort out a payment plan. Do not ignore them and hope that they will go away, along with the debt you owe.

Poor Investment Decisions

Investments always run the risk of losing money. Unless you understand the money market thoroughly, don't try to do this on your own. Investigate the brokerage that you are planning on using thoroughly. Find someone who is able to invest over multiple portfolios so you are not placing all of your eggs (funds) in one basket. That way, should one of your portfolios underperform, the chances of all of them going bottom-up is fairly slim.

Results of Debt

Apart from causing increased levels of anxiety and frustration, which often influence mental health, debt can have a negative influence on relationships. These relationships can be further strained if mental health problems lead to depression. Once again, this can be a vicious cycle that's difficult to break and often leads to separation and divorce amongst couples.

Short-Term Loans

Even short-term loans between paydays are not a good idea. These are often loaded with high interest rates. These should be an absolute last resort.

Sports and Recreational Costs

Making use of funds that you don't necessarily have to purchase sports and recreational equipment, pay gym membership fees, or pay club membership fees if you're a golfer is crazy if you can't afford to eat. In many instances, this starts off in the workplace after someone invites you to join them in one of their favorite pastimes. Before long, you find that you've spent a fortune on fancy equipment that's going to lie in the trunk of your car or sit in your garage most of the year.

Unless you are a serious sports enthusiast or a professional, weigh out all your options before making any extreme purchases. You might even consider finding some used equipment for a fraction of the price that works just as well as brand new equipment.

Unemployment

This can cause major tension in a home regarding finances, especially if the breadwinner of the family is the person who has lost their job. This is often where even the most cautious of individuals begin to burn holes in their credit cards. The longer they are unemployed, the worse this becomes, and once cards are maxed out, it seems like there's nowhere else to go.

Uninformed About Finances

As mentioned in the introduction, not all of us have been fortunate enough to be taught about finances and how to manage them effectively. However, thanks to the internet and Google, there are many ways that you can make a point of educating yourself regarding the subject. If you don't want to go this route, ask around in your social circle for recommendations in regards to financial advisors or bankers who may be able to assist you further.

Weddings

Last, but certainly not least, we come to a hot topic! Here is an example of way too much money being spent on a single event. Young couples should trim the cloth to suit their budget and not try to break the bank, instead. There are many creative ideas regarding ways to still make a wedding day special without breaking the bank in the process. Even if you are the parents of the bride or groom, is it really worth taking a second mortgage out on your property to give your child a single experience that will soon become a distant memory? Is it not wiser to provide them with money instead that they could use for more lasting things, such as a down payment on a house?

Many young couples are opting for simpler ceremonies, cash bars, and homemade décor over wasting thousands on an event that lasts only a few hours.

Why Do People Choose to Stay in Debt?

Everyone knows that debt is bad, so why do they choose to stay in it? Well, there are a few reasons.

When you happen to be stuck in debt, you are too close to the situation, and all that you can see is how far in the hole you really are. Too many people can't seem to see themselves getting out of debt. They believe that it's too big for them to pay off, and so they shrug their shoulders and say, "Why bother?"

Others have become so used to fending off credit card companies that they've mastered the art. They've resigned themselves to the fact that they may need to file for bankruptcy and are prepared to go through this entire process just to have the slate wiped clean.

Here are some more reasons that debt specialist Dave Ramsey shares with us:

Addiction to Gadgets

Individuals struggling with debt are often totally addicted to having the latest gadgets and gizmos, which is why they're not prepared to try to get out of their debt. For them, sacrificing their toys is simply not an option.

Appearances

Similar to keeping up with the Joneses, these people like to "look like everything is going well for them". Although, when you peel back the layers of the onion, they are living on credit, and most of their credit cards are maxed out. They're usually battling to survive, living paycheck to paycheck every month.

Believing Lies

Many individuals deep in the hole believe the lies that they've been fed regarding debt—that there's no way out. Because of this belief, they choose to do nothing (other than to create more debt for themselves). They've resigned themselves to the fact that everyone has debt, and it will always be hanging over them like the sword of Damocles.

Hopelessness

There is a sense of hopelessness that joins the belief that there's no way out. This often leads to a life that's filled with fear and anxiety rather than peace and stability. If you were given a choice and you knew that there was even a glimmer of hope at the end of the tunnel, surely this would make things worth fighting for, right? Fear and hopelessness can rob us of any joy we might possibly have. We need to be aware that like the lie that exists about getting out of debt, believing that your situation is a hopeless one is also completely false.

Ignorance

There's nothing quite like pleading ignorance when it comes to debt. The question needs to be raised, then, as to where you were when the debt was being accrued? We cannot live in a vacuum and pretend that everything is going to be okay. This is where we need to step outside our little bubble that we may have built around ourselves and take full responsibility for the debt that is ours.

It's Not a Priority

Not making getting out of our debt a priority is also a simplistic approach to managing yourself and your life. The longer you wait to begin trying to get yourself out of debt, the deeper your debt pit grows. Working on the assumption that you'll begin tomorrow, at the end of the month, or sometime in the future never works because that time never comes.

There's no time like the present to make changes to the way you're choosing to live your life ("choice" being the operative word). You can make changes to your lifestyle and knock your debt right out of the park from the moment you make the decision that doing so is important. This should become your top priority rather than not a priority at all.

Spousal Relationships

One of the most challenging debt obstacles to overcome is when you and your spouse are not on the same page when it comes to finances and outstanding debt. This is where working on a combined budget can be hugely beneficial. Once you can *both* see where the money is going and *how much* is actually being wasted on frivolous things, it becomes easier to come to a mutual conclusion. You must be prepared to work together on debt that's been acquired (after all, it has probably been both of you spending excessively).

Share everything, and put a plan in place that will help you get rid of your debt together. It will take mutual agreement and keeping one another motivated to resolve your financial problems.

"Unwilling to Sacrifice" Lifestyle

Getting used to living in a certain way is definitely a stumbling block when it comes to remaining in debt. In many ways, this could potentially be what got you there in the first place. Remember the way that Dave and Claire tackled their debt by getting rid of everything that they had no need for? You can do this, too, and use this money toward paying off what you owe.

There are ways of maintaining a comfortable lifestyle without gaining ridiculous amounts of debt. Choosing to live within your means is a wiser decision. Stop unnecessary spending. The only one that your lifestyle choices are hurting is you. One of the first things that Dave and Claire did was cut their credit cards up into tiny little pieces. You can survive off a debit card, and most offer exactly the same functionality of a credit card without having the "credit" option attached.

Debt Pit Trap Design

The main reason that banks and other retail outlets are so quick to offer credit is that by design, it has been created to ensnare people. It's there to keep you locked in as long as possible. The debt pit is more than a hole; it is a designed trap. The government, banks, and credit card companies want you to be in debt.

The statistics of Americans in debt are staggering. According to Forbes, some 75% of Americans are more than $11.5 trillion in debt (yes, you read that correctly—trillions of dollars). This was the figure in 2013, and most of this debt was attached to student loans, car loans, credit card debt, and home mortgages (Touryalai, 2014).

According to the Debt Resistors' Operations Manual, we've been programmed from a young age to feel like being in debt is something to be ashamed about and/or like something we should be punished for. This traditional teaching is flawed, however, because the reality is that everything is actually stacked against you as a debtor.

The entire system has been designed that way. You don't have the power to control any of the major costs mentioned in the Forbes article above; they are controlled by the government. If you're sitting with major medical expenses, it's because there's a limit to how much medical care is provided to citizens in the country, and it's not available to everyone.

The government controls the cost of education and is responsible for driving student loans upwards constantly, making it more and more difficult for those leaving college with qualifications to ever repay what they owe. Banks are also to blame because they are quick to offer loans to students, especially those with no credit. This is done on the premise that they will find work as soon as they graduate, and these loans will be repaid. The reality, however, has been a lot grimmer than this.

High unemployment rates are making it more and more difficult for these graduates to find suitable jobs, and many feel that they would have been better off not going to college at all. This is having a knock-on effect, especially for millennials as they are now buried in debt, and this is stopping them from making lifelong purchasing decisions like buying a home and settling down. The entire system is skewed in favor of the government, banks, and other credit card institutions.

What's even more disconcerting is that credit cards aren't always being used to purchase luxury items. Instead, they're being used to cover day-to-day living expenses such as groceries, gas, and other basic necessities.

There are even alternative financial services (AFS) that offer credit outside the conventional banking industry, and about 9 million Americans take advantage of these services rather than opening a checking account. The problem with these is that they are offered at much higher interest rates than normal, and there are many other hidden costs and fees that you don't always see at first.

The Credit Card Revolution

The first-ever credit card was introduced in 1950 by Diner's Club. This was believed to be the brainchild of Ralph Schneider and Frank McNamara. While this was not technically a credit card, whatever you happened to spend with the card became payable in full at the end of each month. If we were to compare it to today's standards, this was very similar to the way that current debit cards work, only with a delayed payment option at the end of each month.

The Bank of America was the next to release what was known as BankAmericard to 60,000 homes in Fresno, California. This small piece of plastic was about to unleash the power of credit into every home in the area. Americans suddenly held in their hands purchasing power that they'd never experienced before. Where they would have had to save for months or even years before, now they could simply swipe for whatever they wanted. Within two years, these cardholders had amassed a total of almost $60 million of debt.

This card would soon transform into what we refer to as Visa today. The credit revolution had started in earnest, and individuals became dependent on simply putting things on their card (instant gratification). In the early days of Visa, it was more likely that high ticket items such as televisions and furniture were swiped onto credit cards, while some 70 years later, you will find that cards are now being used to pay for a $5 café latte.

Prior to the invention and introduction of the credit card, you would need to schedule an appointment with the bank to secure a short- or long-term loan. This would often give people the time to think about what they really wanted and whether they actually needed to take out a loan. There was a process that needed to be followed which was far lengthier than the one that must be gone through to get a piece of plastic conveniently mailed to you.

The downside of all of this is that millennials are getting sucked into a revolving credit trap when it comes to cards being issued to them freely. Students are initially being offered a card (which many intend on using only for emergencies). Low thresholds ensure that the debt can't get out of hand, and so most can stay on top of paying their monthly installments. This is not the way the system was designed, though.

The moment you have one card, it seems as though you are likely to be offered multiple cards at the same time. This is where the spending goes a bit haywire, ultimately getting out of hand. What was once manageable to repay is now a massive amount of money. There's a huge difference between a credit cap of $2,000 or $3,000 and $25,000 or $30,000. Can you see how the credit revolution is designed to keep you a slave to your debt?

While this may have all started off as 60,000 cards being delivered to each household in Fresno in 1958, it has now been blown way out of proportion with a massive 3.67 billion cards in circulation in 2016—and counting. The goal for the banks and financial institutions is to keep the money circulating through the economy. However, what is meant to stimulate the economy can very easily backfire horribly as was made apparent by the housing crisis in 2008. In fact, in the event that the credit industry collapses, it's likely to make the housing crisis look like child's play.

Chapter 3:

Stop Digging

"If you find yourself in a hole, stop digging." ~ Will Rogers.

There are usually a number of reasons you might find yourself in a debt pit every month. One of these reasons is that you are spending more than you make which, in turn, is creating a monthly deficit; instead of being able to live off your paycheck and still have money left over at the end of each month, you reach for your credit cards to fund the deficit. The second reason is that you have no savings in reserve for emergency situations. Once again, in the event that you're faced with something that's not planned for, your credit card becomes the quick-fix solution.

Here are some practical steps that will help you stop digging that pit even deeper and start building a ladder that leads you out of it instead.

Become Informed

Instead of making your debt situation worse by ignoring it, learn as much as you can about each of your debts. This includes owning up to what your principal debt is, as well as the interest rate per account. It's important to realize that pleading ignorance doesn't work and only makes matters worse when it comes to owing money. Students are particularly prone to being in debt as they continue to take more and more loans while they complete numerous degrees—some of these loan totals even hitting six figures.

It's much better to know exactly what you owe and to whom you owe it, down to the very last dollar. Reality can be a bitter pill to swallow, but it's better once the medicine actually goes down and you have a starting point where you can begin to make some sort of difference when it comes to what you owe. Remember to include *everything* and *everyone* you owe money to.

Catch Up Default Accounts

If you know that some of your accounts are currently in default, before you start working on any other payment plans, commit to getting these up-to-date as quickly as possible. Once you have done this, you can begin setting up a repayment plan that works for you.

Cut Up All Your Credit Cards

Get rid of all further temptation to put things on credit. This includes retail credit cards for clothing, furniture, or other services. Find a decent pair of scissors, cut those pesky pieces of plastic into tiny bits, and throw them away. Replace your credit cards with a single debit card. The beauty of this is that unless you actually have the cash in your account, you cannot overspend. This will definitely prevent you from spending impulsively. It may take you a month or so to get used to this way of living, but at least you will know that you're not incurring any further debt that is part of a "buy now, pay later" scheme.

Minimize Living Expenses

Cut back on everything that's not an absolute necessity. This includes groceries, lifestyle costs (such as eating out), family vacations, "toys" for recreational purposes (bikes, boats, jet-skis, and anything in between). If you can't afford to pay for these things in cash or make regular use of them, try to get rid of all this excess "stuff" via platforms like eBay, Craigslist, or Facebook Marketplace.

Instead of a garden service, take over this responsibility yourself. You'd be amazed at how much you can cut back on your current monthly expenditure. Shop around for the best prices rather than adding the first item you come across on your shopping list. Finally, work strictly according to your budget.

Building a Budget

Putting a detailed budget together is definitely one of the first things that you should be doing. This will show you where the money is going. A simple technique that can assist you in sticking to this budget is to physically divide all your expenses up into separate envelopes with the cash amount that you're prepared to spend for the month inside. Once that amount is spent, that's it!

Admittedly, this process takes a bit of getting used to, but it can be ideal for smaller debts or utility bills that need to be paid. This technique can also become a way to force yourself to save a percentage of your income each month.

Your budget will allow you to track where your money is going every month. Draw up a spreadsheet where you can add every purchase that you make, and allocate it to a specific area (just like a bookkeeper would do). In the event that you find that you're short every month, you may need to take on extra work to supplement your income monthly. The most important part of your budget is working out how to cut back on your spending. If a large chunk of your money is being allocated towards luxuries, you may need to sacrifice these to the point where there's money left at the end of each month.

While setting up your budget, it is worthwhile to put a detailed income and expenditure spreadsheet together. The first things that should appear on this list should be your necessities—those things that you simply *have* to pay for each month. This will include expenses like your rent or mortgage, car repayments, or travel expenses if you commute with public transportation. Utility costs also cannot be avoided nor can clothing, food, and gas.

When you have all of this information in front of you, think about what you can do to cut back on some of these expenses. If you find that your rent or mortgage is more than a quarter of your current income, then it may be time to consider finding somewhere that's cheaper.

Setting Up a Budget

We've discussed drawing up a budget for yourself to help manage your finances better, but you may have no idea what this involves or where to begin. The following information should help you with any questions that you may have in this regard and help you get started right away. Your budget will show you where the bulk of your money is going, and that will give you the opportunity to alter your spending habits or make some tough financial decisions. This is because now you will be at least working with accurate numbers, rather than with finances you *think* you have.

Step 1: Know Why You Want a Budget

Drawing up a budget for the sake of a budget is not reason enough to keep you motivated to either stick with it or make use of it correctly. Identifying where the bulk of your money is going each month will highlight areas of overspending such as "eating out" or "clothing accounts". There are a number of reasons that you might have for wanting to put a budget together. Some of these might include the following:

- Maybe your allocation to housing is too rich for your current budget, which could suggest that finding somewhere more affordable should be considered if you are presently renting. You will be amazed at what you discover when you really start digging compared with what you're presently assuming.

- You may be looking for additional disposable income to repay your debts and get rid of them a lot more quickly than you're currently doing. A proper budget will show you where you can possibly cut back on some of your regular spending to do so.
- Saving for a new car or a new home may be your main motivation for having a budget, or you may be expecting a new addition to the family, and you know this will require some proper planning and extra money.
- Your reasoning also could be medically related. Perhaps you have bills outstanding that need to be met.

The bottom line is this: whatever your reason for creating this budget might be, it's something that will be personal to you. Ask yourself the really difficult financial questions so that your budget can work for you.

If you are hoping to save money, how much money and by what date (be specific with both the amount of money and your dates). You might even want to break this larger final figure down into reasonable chunk sizes that you can manage monthly without having to skimp too badly. Being specific is the secret to the success of your budget.

Be sure that your goals are realistic. It doesn't help to commit to saving $500 each month when there's already a shortfall and you're currently living paycheck to paycheck.

By changing how you live, you may be able to trim down some of your living expenses and save $100 each month. While this seems to fall dramatically short of the idealistic $500, if you do this consistently each month, these figures will compound and begin to grow nicely, albeit at a slower rate. Being tenacious and not giving up are the keys to being able to save within even the tightest of budgets.

Budgeting may be something completely new to you. Below is a straightforward, no-nonsense way to set up a simple monthly budget.

Step 2: Income and Expenses

To put it simply, budgets are divided into two separate components: money coming in and money going out.

You can either write this down over two pages or set up a spreadsheet on the computer. The beauty of working from a spreadsheet is that you can set it up so that all the figures change automatically rather than having to do it manually.

Start by considering and capturing ALL of your income, including passive income sources, income that you may receive as part of rental agreements, income from a second job, or inheritances. Capture all of this information under **INCOME**.

On the opposite side of the page, or several columns over if working in Excel, you can add another heading for **EXPENSES** or **EXPENDITURE**.

It might be a bit tricky to find different sub-headings at first. An excellent way of starting with this process is by pulling out bank statements.

The aim of this exercise is to group your expenses into different categories. Examples of this might include the following: "mortgage/rent and utilities"; "insurance(s)" (this would include all insurance premiums or policies that you are paying, some of which might include life insurance, homeowners insurance, insurance against loans, medical insurance, motor vehicle insurance, funeral plans, and so on). Lump all of your insurance costs together, and write this total figure down.

Next comes any loan agreements; these I would keep separate because they may each be on different terms. Loan agreements would include the following:

- Credit card accounts
- Clothing store accounts
- Retail accounts
- Student loan accounts
- Vehicle loan accounts

- Bank charges
- All other personal loans or revolving credit loans

Add a subheading for **LIVING EXPENSES**. Under this heading, include the following:

- Phone accounts (include any fixed landlines to ALL mobile accounts). If these vary depending on the data used, calculate an average over the last three to six months by consulting your bank statements.

- Internet and/or Wi-Fi (same as above; if costs vary from month to month, capture an average amount).

- Groceries (this is also likely to vary from month to month. Do your best to get an average cost).

- Dining out and entertainment. This would exclude home-based entertainment such as pay-per-view channels, Netflix, or any other entertainment channel (this should be another line item).

- Home entertainment (Netflix, PPV channels, or other syndicated networks, including cable).

- Gasoline and/or transportation. Whether you're making use of the public bus, trains, trams, or

Uber, include all your transportation costs for the month.

- Clothing. This would be anything purchased with cash that's not on a credit card or retail card.

- Medical expenses. This includes your out-of-pocket expenses for medication and visits to doctors or hospitals that are not covered by your health insurance. Remember that you have already included your actual health insurance under the "insurance" section.

These expenses are usually fixed. This means that they don't change from month to month. Include all bank charges in these expenses as well.

Education

This category should include any and all education-related expenses. If you're paying for a private tutor or your children are attending private schools that have tuition fees, include these here. Any additional expenses linked to extracurricular activities like dancing or archery should also be included in this section, but these should be listed under separate line items.

Savings

Include any savings that you might be putting away each month in this category.

Donations

This category can include regular donations that you make to your church in the form of tithes and offerings, a regular donation to Greenpeace, for example, or a fund to feed orphaned children.

Scan through your bank statements to see whether there happens to be anything that you may have missed. Include this in the same format as above by grouping as many similar expenses together.

Living Out

If you happen to travel for business, you may need to pay for your own meals for these to be reimbursed by the company on your return. Be sure to keep accurate records of all of your expenses and reimbursements. They can be included in this category.

Miscellaneous

Check through your statements to find out whether there is anything that you've missed. Several other expenses may include monthly subscriptions to magazines, you might pay Amazon for their Audible service or their Amazon's Kindle Unlimited service. All of these things come out of your account automatically each month. You may be paying for a gym membership or other membership fees you were not aware of. Capture each of these under a subheading titled "Memberships".

Final Step: Reviewing Your Expenses

Once you have each of these headings in place, it's time to begin adding all the figures in to determine whether you come out in the red or black for the month. If you're currently in a nasty debt trap, chances are your budget will appear to be more red than black.

This is where some brutal decisions need to be made. What do you absolutely need, and what can you begin to cut back on? Some of your expenses will be classified as "fixed expenses". This means that you have to pay them every month, and the amounts are usually exactly the same from month to month. These are the debts that you can't change or get out of.

There is a suggested model budget that is known as 50/30/20. This recommends that 50% of your income is allocated to fixed expenses and other needs. Needs are things that you simply cannot go without. 30% is allocated to your wants (this could include things like clothing, shoes, and luxury items), and the remaining 20% should be earmarked for savings.

This model is obviously to be used in an ideal world and not one where you are facing mountains of debt. However, if you're able to get your needs covered by 50% of your income, essentially by trimming your "cloth right down", you could potentially have anywhere between 20 to 50% of your income freed up to settle outstanding debts.

This would mean initially sacrificing your wants and your savings for a period of time, but once you've managed to make a significant dent in what you owe your creditors, you can revert to this model or keep playing with the percentages until you are focused on getting completely out of debt.

Set Up a Savings Account

Unexpected emergencies happen whether we want to admit it or not. The most important thing is for us to be prepared as much as possible. Setting up a savings account into which you can set money aside on a regular basis is something that's worthwhile to get into the habit of doing. The ideal amount should be between one and three months worth of net income. This may take you a while to set aside, but slow, consistent effort will pay off at the end of the day. This money will help you out of any major emergency situation that you might be faced with.

When you are in the debt pit, you are usually quite aware of your current situation, even when you choose to ignore it. There are ways to prevent further pressure and anxiety but only if you begin to take control of your own financial situation. There is no time to waste debating this or trying to find ways around it. There's only one way to get over debt and that's going through all the pain of the repayment process. The good news, though, is that it is definitely possible.

Another reason for saving is for any large purchase that you know you're going to need in the future. While you will have the satisfaction of being able to put the entire amount down for these items, you will really appreciate them because you've saved for them rather than simply swiping your card and enjoying that moment of instant gratification. Saving gives you time to really shop around for the best prices as well. You will have the time to search for quality at a good price, rather than settling for an impulse buy because your credit card is burning a hole in your pocket.

Set Up Payment Plans

Set up a debt payment plan by setting aside enough money to make a dent in your debt. This plan will allow you to see exactly what you owe each debtor. It will also make it crystal-clear how quickly you might be able to turn things around for yourself. Another key to payment plans is having the discipline to see these plans through no matter how unmotivated you get. Having a visual representation of how you're doing when it comes to paying off your debt is a great reminder as to why you should stay motivated and keep moving forward.

Getting out of debt is not easy, and there's no quick fix or simple way to do it. Consider what you will be able to do with all the money that you're currently paying someone else once your debt has finally been settled.

You can add this amount to your savings or seriously consider participating in financial investments.

Other Solutions

You've accepted that you're in the pit and have the tools to slowly begin digging your way out. Ways to cut back on your expenses include cooking at home instead of buying take-out, shopping for special deals (possibly saving a little each month to buy in bulk at discounted prices), and looking for second-hand deals (this could be anything from furniture to cars to clothing and anything in between. Set aside additional income that you may receive in the form of bonuses, tax refunds, income from other jobs, funds received from goods sold, etc., and use this money toward repaying debt; do not use it to purchase extravagant luxury items.

The main thing is to stop getting yourself deeper into debt. Each of the above methods is a sure way to get out of the hole. You can decide which applies specifically to your situation as the choice always remains in your hands. I would recommend that you start with the income and expenditure sheet and move on to a budget. These can easily be generated in a spreadsheet program where they can be accessed and monitored with just a few clicks of the mouse.

You may be pleasantly surprised to discover exactly how much money you can save by tightening your budget or shopping around for the best prices. Stop delaying making changes to your current financial situation, for each day you stall the more compound interest your debt will accrue.

Chapter 4:

Dealing With Creditors

"While I encourage people to save 100 % down for a home, a mortgage is the one debt that I don't frown upon." ~ Dave Ramsey

Get Creditors Off Your Back Without Losing Your Shirt

Receiving all of those irritating calls from debt collectors can really put a total damper on your day. The good news is that there are ways of dealing with them that can actually work in your favor. In this chapter, we are going to investigate what creditors and collection agencies can and can't do as well as the legal rights of both parties. It pays to be as educated as possible so you know when you're being bullied into something that you shouldn't be.

Even though you may be sick of these calls, there are a couple of reasons why you should be prepared to answer them. Occasionally the original creditors are prepared to negotiate with you, because that way they don't need to be inconvenienced by having to pay a collection agency to do the job for them.

If you can, try to imagine for one moment that you are a college or university, and you have hundreds or even thousands of default accounts. Paying a collection agency a fee on each of these accounts can add up to be a fairly hefty sum of money. The same goes for a financial institution that is trying to obtain credit card debt they are owed. With the number of defaulters out there, the additional payments could mean that they receive very little of the principal debt (original outstanding amount).

Selling of Default Debt

Depending on how old the debt is, some of these collection agencies are able to pick up outstanding debt for next to nothing. This is great news for you because should this be the case, they're usually prepared to settle for a much lower rate than the original outstanding amount is. As long as they make a profit on what they paid for the principal debt, they're happy. When we talk about them buying this debt, it's literally for a couple of pennies on the dollar.

Last-Ditch Attempts by Creditors

Before your debt even reaches a collection agency, the creditor may be willing to settle for something, rather than being forced to write the entire debt off completely.

In the event that any of the above settlements are reached, make sure that you take a lot of notes, and ensure that once you settle the debt, you receive a note stating that the debt has been settled. This prevents it from reappearing somewhere else where they have no record of your payments, and you may find yourself being forced to pay off the same debt for a second time.

Even when they tell you that all calls are recorded, it's worthwhile confirming your current financial situation with them via email at the end of each and every conversation that you have with them. Be sure to keep all this correspondence in a place that is easy for you to access whenever you need it.

There are several ways you can enter into negotiations with collection agencies or creditors, which are detailed below.

Arrange for Communications to Be Sent to You

Keep copies of all communications and correspondence so you can refer back to them in the event of a dispute. This is especially important when you've come to a payment arrangement. Keep accurate notes on all agreements and how long they're likely to be in place. That way, even if another creditor calls you, you can refer to previous discussions.

Be Honest About Your Present Situation

While it may be true that creditors and/or credit controllers listen to sob stories all day long, this is actually their job that they are being paid for. Be completely honest about your current financial situation and why you are unable to afford to pay your outstanding accounts. Telling the truth is a key ingredient when dealing with these people, because whether we like it or not, the truth will always find a way of coming to light. It also makes things so much worse when you begin lying about your ability to repay your debts.

Some of the reasons why you are in your current situation may be that you've undergone major surgery and had an extensive recovery period where you've been unable to work, or perhaps you or your spouse may have lost your job, cutting your household income down substantially. You may have just had a baby and been on maternity leave with a fraction of your income being paid out, yet your cost of living has suddenly increased because having an infant is way more expensive than you could imagine, especially your first child.

Explain your situation to your creditors, and either ask for a deferment or payment holiday for a couple of months while you try to get back on your feet, or try to form an arrangement with them that you know you can manage financially.

Credit Counselors

If you are really battling with large sums of outstanding debt and you don't know where to turn, it may be worthwhile finding a debt counselor who can give you sound advice on how to go about repaying accounts. They may be able to help you plan your repayments, especially when you owe several individuals. When searching for credit counselors, ask to be referred to someone who has a track record of helping individuals get out of debt. The last thing you need is to be given advice from some smooth-talking hack who actually has no experience in the industry.

Don't Overcommit

If you've completed an income and expenditure statement, as well as a monthly budget, you should have a fairly good idea of how much money you can afford to allocate to repayments each month. Be honest with each of your creditors about the facts in regards to what you have available to contribute. If you make a commitment to pay a specific amount of money each month, then be sure to do so. In the event that something comes up that prevents you from making the payment for the month, notify them in advance; it's worthwhile keeping the lines of communication open.

Keep Records

Keep accurate records of everything—not just your calls and communications with your creditor(s) or collection agencies, but also all your payments. It's easy for certain payments to slip through the cracks. Be sure that you attach the correct reference number(s) to each of your payments so that they can be allocated to the right account. By keeping accurate records (even a phone screenshot of the bank transaction), you can send this through to them in the event of a dispute.

Because some of these payments (especially credit card debt and/or student loan accounts) can often take many years to pay off, it's worthwhile saving all of this information in one place. Technology makes this easier to do. You can also keep copies of all your bank statements where payments have been made to various accounts. This may be an easier way to file this information should it ever be needed in the event of a dispute.

Leave the Past in the Past

Try to pay off your debts as quickly as possible. Once they've been resolved, request your creditor to remove any outstanding poor credit reports from the credit bureau for you. In some instances, you may be able to do this yourself with a letter from the debtor. Failure to do so could result in you having a poor credit rating hanging over your head for several years.

This could affect not only your future credit rating, but it may exclude you from purchasing a home, buying a car, or getting additional credit elsewhere. The ideal situation is to try to clear away all bad ratings as quickly as possible.

Remain Calm

When dealing with either the creditor directly or a collection agency, it really doesn't help to get hot and bothered or aggressive with these individuals over the phone. After all, they are only doing what they are supposed to. If you paid attention to the earlier sections, you should have realized that you are most likely the person to be held accountable for the debt that you've agreed to pay. The moment that you become aggressive with them or that they become aggressive with you, you should end the call or ask for someone else to call you back.

There are undoubtedly times when certain personalities clash. This is one of the last things that you need, however, as you want to be able to negotiate with a clear head. People cannot come to a compromise when they are excitable or in a bad headspace.

Remain Informed

Keep abreast of the industry and the law when it comes to both creditors and collection agencies. There are certain things that they are allowed to do and other things that they can't do. Do yourself a favor, and become aware of all the ins and outs pertaining to what is allowed. This will prevent them from walking all over you or bullying you into a corner. While they may be doing their jobs, there's no need for them to be emotional or aggressive with you. It is not their money that they're collecting; it is for and on behalf of the creditor, at the end of the day.

Try the Creditor Directly

It's always best to negotiate with the creditor directly. After all, the principal debt and agreement was made with them. In many instances, they are prepared to write off a portion of the debt to be able to get something back, rather than having to sell the debt off for a fraction of what it's actually worth. They end up losing a lot of money when they don't come to an amicable arrangement that works for both parties.

Legal Advice

When it comes to the laws surrounding debt owed, you should know as much as possible. This way, you can keep yourself safe from being taken advantage of, and you will have the knowledge to get yourself out of debt more quickly. Thus, you can read on to learn about what the legal experts advise in addition to the information above.

Dealing with Banks/Financial Institutions

One of the most important things to do is to set up an appointment with the financial institution directly. Make the appointment with the right person. This can be either the branch manager, the loans manager, or even your personal banker (if you have one of these). Go into the branch and meet with them face to face. Be prepared with all the necessary documentation. If you've been laid off, take copies of all company documents proving that you no longer have work or a fixed income.

Take a copy of your income and expenses so they can see where your money is going each month. This will also give them an idea of how much disposable income you have to restructure your debt.

If you know that you cannot pay the full amount and it will keep gathering interest, there are a couple of options at your disposal. First, you can ask for a portion of the debt to be written off (this is better than you filing for bankruptcy and them getting nothing). Please note that student loans fall out of the bankruptcy purview, and you will always be responsible for this (thanks to the government).

You also have the option of asking them to forego additional interest on the principal amount. This means that they stop adding interest to the account (which may make it easier for you to repay).

Offer them a settlement amount as a once-off payment that they can either accept or reject; if the latter occurs, neither party really wins. Should the reason for non-payment be medically related, you can provide them with proof of this, and request that the debt be written off or forgiven.

Remember to be honest with them regarding your situation. The moment they feel that you may be lying to them, they will immediately hand the debt over to a collection agency or sell it to other collection houses at a fraction of the initial debt.

Dealing with Collection Agencies

Be sure that the collection agency you are dealing with is operating within the confines of the law. There are specific collection and debt settlement acts that dictate exactly how these agencies should be doing things. One of the first things is that they should be mailing you all of the relevant information regarding who the creditor is, the principal amount that is outstanding, and the authorization that they have to be acting on behalf of the creditor.

You have six days to respond before they can make contact with you.

Once they contact you, you can attempt to negotiate with them much like you would with the principal creditor. Be sure to keep accurate records of all interactions with the collection agency.

In the event that a collection agency is harassing you, there are certain courses of action that can be taken. These are as follows:

- You can provide them with a registered letter disputing the debt and recommending that the matter be taken to court.

- If your lawyer makes contact with them, you can also provide them with a registered letter requesting that all communication be channeled through the lawyer.

- You can bring to their attention that you are not the person responsible for the account if this is the case.

There are a whole host of other things that collection agencies are not allowed to do, but these laws change from state to state or country to country. It's worthwhile to educate yourself concerning the laws governing your region or country.

Agreements

Should you make a payment arrangement with the collection agency, in exactly the same way as we've indicated above, place everything in writing and keep accurate records of exactly what was agreed upon, when it was agreed upon, when it comes into effect, or the duration of the agreement, as well as any other proof of negotiations.

This agreement should be signed by both parties before you commit to making any payments.

Never pay a collection agency in cash. It's best to always have a paper trail of bank deposits or canceled checks.

Understanding Debt Collectors

Buyers of Debt

This is a last-ditch attempt for creditors to recover at least something on the outstanding debt. Groups of debt of a certain value are sold off at an extremely low rate of $0.04 or $0.05 per dollar. The main reason the price is so low is due to the fact that a great deal of the debt is unrecoverable, and so whatever they manage to collect is a bonus. The disadvantage for these companies is that the debt can be so old that they have no idea where it came from or exactly how old it is. This is often when they run into a brick wall by making contact with the wrong people.

There's a lot of work that goes into trying to track and trace the correct individuals responsible for the debt, and only then can the negotiations begin (all over again).

Collection Agencies

When creditors can't seem to be making headway with you, they may finally appoint a collection agency to handle the debt on their behalf. This is not in their best interest, because their fees can range from between 25 and 60% of the debt collected. This is why debt collection agencies can often be rude and pushy. It's in their best interest to bleed you dry, because the more money they're able to collect from you, the more money they make themselves. These organizations are highly regulated, though, and this is where it pays to become informed as to what they can and can't do.

Internal Departments

Here, you are dealing with an internal department of the actual organization that originally provided you with the loan or line of credit. Because they are a division of the organization, they will usually be polite and accommodating. It's in their best interest to try to come to a payment arrangement with you, even if it is only a partial payment. The main reason for this is that they then don't need to pay the collection agents the hefty commission fees as indicated above or sell off the principal amount for pennies on the dollar.

Chapter 5:

Climb Out

"Self-reliance cannot be obtained when there is serious debt hanging over a household. One has neither independence nor freedom from bondage when he is obligated to others." ~ Gordon B. Hinckley

So by now, you should have cut up your credit cards and switched over to a single debit card instead. All your clothing and retail store accounts should now be closed as well. Also, unnecessary monthly subscriptions should be canceled. At this point, you should be managing to stay away from anything that's going to put you into further debt, and you should have set up some repayment plans with creditors and/or collection agencies so they aren't hounding you day and night for payments.

The time has come to put some serious repayment plans into place to actually climb out of the debt pit you're in rather than taking a few steps out and sliding back in. In this chapter, we're going to cover some effective methods to help you get out of both long- and short-term debt.

These strategies are certain to result in short-term pain and discomfort as you will have to change your lifestyle. However, this is necessary to solve your debt crisis. Remember your main motivation in Chapter 1? There is only one way to get out of debt for good, and that's to power your way through it and climb out of the pit.

Debt guru Dave Ramsey recommends several ways to get out of debt when you're faced with significant long-term debts. He provides a proven method that he has been using for more than a quarter of a century, helping those who face the challenge of digging their way out of the debt pit. According to Ramsey, the first step is to save $1,000 as an emergency fund. This may prove to be relatively difficult, especially in a single-income household where you're already living paycheck to paycheck.

Remember in Chapter 1 when Dave and Claire managed to set aside these funds by selling some of their "recreational toys" on eBay? Consider what you already have in your home. Are you sitting on a goldmine of stuff that you've accumulated over the years that could quite easily bring in this kind of money? If not, consider a side hustle or finding a second job for a while so you can earn it.

His second piece of advice is to begin using his "snowball" method of paying off your debts. Here's how to go about it:

Draw up a comprehensive list of all your debts, irrespective of the interest rate(s) attached to them. Arrange this list from your smallest to biggest debt. Begin paying these debts off by being aggressive in repaying your smallest debt. You should continue to pay the minimum amounts due on each of your other accounts each month. Once the smallest debt has been fully repaid, move on to the next debt by adding whatever you were paying on the first debt to the current repayment installments due (this is what it means to be aggressive in repaying your outstanding debt).

Continue this process until you have managed to get rid of all your debt. The only debt that Dave considers worthwhile is your mortgage. If this is your only debt left, it's worth paying more on your monthly repayments as this will bring your interest rates down significantly. Also, you will be able to pay your mortgage off in a fraction of the term, saving yourself a bundle of money in unnecessary interest (Ramsey, n.d.).

Cut Costs Through Frugal Living

There are several other ways to cut your living expenses down to almost the bone and allocate whatever you manage to save toward debt. Take a look below at some of the things you can start doing today to save money.

Avoid Café's and Coffee Shops

You would be surprised by how much your favorite coffee shop or corner café is actually costing you each month. Consider how much you are spending, and instead invest in decent coffee or cappuccino that can be bought with your groceries. You will find that this alone will lead to significant savings. Use this extra money to go toward alleviating your debt.

Avoid Eating Out

It's much too quick and convenient to hop into the car and hit your nearest drive-through or family restaurant. When you really think about what you spend and what you are actually getting in return, the cons certainly outweigh the pros. Yes, you may not have to wash the dishes and clear away the kitchen, but is taking away this minor inconvenience really worth what you spend on taking your entire family out for a meal?

Avoid Investments

Place all your investments on hold until you are completely out of the hole. This may seem like a strange piece of advice, especially when we're advocating that you still try to save, but it actually makes sense if you are in debt. Once you're completely debt-free, you can always begin reinvesting again. By the time you're finally clear, you will have even more disposable income to invest, quickly catching up from any perceived shortfall while you're still in debt.

Break Up with Your Friends

All of the fake friends that you've spent most of your time trying to keep up with are really just as broke as you. It's time to cut them loose and focus on getting yourselves out of the hole. In the future, you will be enjoying your financial freedom while they are still up to their necks in debt. If you feel like you need to impress certain people, they're not genuine friends that are worth having lifelong associations with.

Check Your Community Pages

Communities often advertise free activities, markets, concerts, and various events that could quite easily serve as a replacement for the entertainment you're currently paying for. Scan Facebook sites and your community news for events that could be happening close to you. If you're fortunate enough to live somewhere scenic or close to the sea, it's worthwhile taking a drive to visit museums, beaches, mountains, or even to go on daytime hikes that aren't going to cost you anything other than maybe a few dollars in gas.

Collect Coupons/Loyalty Cards

People have been doing this for years. Many retail outlets offer discounts via loyalty cards. Whichever is most convenient for you, choose the outlets where immediate discounts are offered, and always compare prices (even when it comes to grocery items). This may involve shopping in several different places, but the savings on your finances will make it all worthwhile.

Don't fall into the trap of buying products that are cheap but that aren't things that you or your family are used to eating. The chances are these items will be wasted as you will probably never use them.

Discuss Finances with Your Family

Let your family know that you're trying to get out of debt and that everyone will need to make certain lifestyle changes. Give them the freedom to discuss any ideas involving ways that everyone can do their bit to help. Kids are more perceptive than we give them credit, and they can often come up with creative ideas to help with finances.

Ditch Expensive Hobbies

There are always those hobbies that cost an arm and a leg. If you do happen to participate in these, it may be in your best interest to put them on hold until you're out of the financial crisis you're currently in. Some of these hobbies might include golf, any sport where there are competitions that require hefty entrance fees or activities that need you to purchase expensive equipment.

If you're using these hobbies as a form of release from the stress you're currently under, take up an alternative that doesn't cost anything. Examples of these are running, hiking, photography (if you already own a camera), reading, meditating, and even gardening. These are all activities that can prove to relieve stress and tension.

Envelopes

This is a method that one of my daughter's taught me. Having spent some time overseas, she was forced to be cautious with the money she had available to her each month, and she began using envelopes for various things. She would work out her budget for the month and physically divide cash for different things into each of the envelopes.

An example of this would be setting aside $100 for utilities for the month, the $100 would be put inside an envelope marked "utilities". Her grocery money would be split into however many weeks were in the month, so she knew that she was on a weekly budget. Whatever wasn't spent throughout the month went into an "emergency/savings" fund.

I was fascinated that a young 22-year-old could actually be so financially astute about working cautiously with her finances.

Find a Second Job

Even if this is for the duration of trying to repay your outstanding debts, look for additional ways to make money. For some people, this involves taking on a second or even third job to supplement income. One example of this is to join freelancing sites and offer your services there. It is, of course, ideal to get onto ones that don't ask for you to put money down to belong to the site, but these are rapidly becoming fewer and fewer. Try your community pages, and offer your services.

Some more ways that you may be able to make some additional money include house-sitting (especially during seasonal holidays), dog-walking, and babysitting. If you're creative and have an eye for detail, you may want to offer your services as a photographer.

Holiday destinations are often looking for waitrons. Although this is often hard work, if you find the right destination with enough tourists, you can make a fair amount of money.

Get Rid of Cable

Cut off your cable, and spend more time together as a family. Your quality of life will change tremendously, and between catching up on reading and taking up hobbies that don't cost as much, you can survive without having your time wasted by the media.

Skip the Gym

Give up your gym membership (only if you're not signed in to a fixed-term contract). The last thing you need is yet another creditor banging your door down! If you are signed into a contract that you really are unable to get out of, then make sure that you use it, and when the time comes for renewal, allow the contract to lapse.

Be sure to read the fine print to make sure that you don't need to give them notice, or confirm in writing that you will not be renewing your agreement. Many of these facilities have an "auto renewal" clause. The last thing you need is to find yourself signed up for another year or two.

Give to Others

There's no better feeling than donating your time and talents to help others (especially when you're not feeling great about yourself). Once again, turn to your local community pages and see whether there are any places that may need your assistance.

There may be a children's hospital near you or a hospice where people are desperately in need of some human interaction. There are social groups that volunteer to make baby clothes for premature babies or knitting socks and beanies for the homeless. There are even organizations that plant trees and deal with wildlife rehabilitation. There's almost certainly something out there that will be of interest to you.

Look for Better Employment

Put your feelers out for better employment where your bring-home pay is better than what you're currently making, or approach your boss and ask for a raise. There's the old adage that goes like this: "If you don't ask, you don't get!"

You never know—your current employer may not want to lose you. Once you explain to them why you need the additional income, they will either agree to it or reject it. So, what do you really have to lose?

Renew Your Library Membership

Instead of spending a fortune on Amazon, look for opportunities to read for free. Almost every town or city has at least one library where you are able to check out several books at a time. In addition to this, there are plenty of apps and sites from which you can download books for free.

Get back into the habit of reading. It can be used as a means of self-development and self-improvement or for entertainment. The upside is that you can also use the library to get books for your children, and they can also develop a love for books from an early age.

Secondhand Clothing Outlets

There are a number of these types of clothing outlets all over the place. Some specialize in pre-loved garments; others offer brand new stock that comes from boutiques and other fashion houses but that are either end-of-range or they've had excess stock in certain sizes.

The chances of finding exactly what you are looking for in one of these stores is almost guaranteed, and because the designer labels have been cut out of the garments, they are usually sold at massively discounted prices.

Sell Your Car

This is a major decision and one that should not be made lightly. This should depend on the age of your vehicle and the monthly repayments. If you are way behind on your payments, then it may be worthwhile to sell your vehicle in order to settle the debt completely. This, however, won't solve a transportation problem.

If you happen to live in the suburbs and are far from any form of public transportation, then this might not be such a great idea. Also, if you and your partner work in opposite directions this might be a bad choice.

As a short-term solution, this may work, however, only if you're able to manage with one car. You could always save up to purchase the next vehicle with cash, though this may not be a new car.

Shop According to a Grocery List

Rather than shopping up and down every aisle in your local Wal-Mart, go to the store with a shopping list of items that you need. This will stop you from overspending on unnecessary items. There's nothing quite as frustrating as shopping and getting home only to discover that you already have toilet paper for the next six months packed in cupboards.

Keep a list handy where you can keep items listed that are gone or almost gone. If you are really feeling energetic, you can actually generate a proper shopping list of everything that you could possibly purchase in a month. At the end of the month, you can highlight or underline those things that you really need and only shop according to that list.

We mentioned checking prices against several stores to ensure that you're getting the best possible deal. This is one of the beauties of technology today—you can shop around quite easily. It's possible for you to even purchase online and get things shipped straight to you for a small delivery fee.

This will definitely prevent you from being tempted by things that you certainly don't need right now. Most of these online department stores are prepared to accept debit cards, so there's no reason to even carry cash around with you.

Quicker Ways to Get Out of Debt

If you'd like to try and tackle your debt much quicker, here are some other suggestions that you may want to try. There's no such thing as a "one size fits all" approach to getting out of debt. What works for one individual, couple, or family doesn't necessarily work for someone else.

These are meant to be short-term solutions, so they may be easier to manage for a couple of months if you're trying to really scale back on your debts.

Avoid Addictions

We're all aware of the conventional addictions that people have such as tobacco and alcohol. These do nothing positive for you when you're already in debt. It's no use preaching to the choir as far as knowledge is concerned that these addictive substances are harmful to your body. What most don't say is that if you're in the habit of stopping for cappuccinos every morning and afternoon and stopping for lunch at the local pub each afternoon with your colleagues, followed again by drinks after work, all of these things are addictive behaviors. In most instances, each of these activities are swiped for and paid for using one of your credit cards.

The solution to this is simple: just STOP! Take pre-packed lunches to work, quit smoking and drinking, and avoid the party crowd of colleagues. This is not to say that you need to suddenly become totally isolated and unfriendly toward people who exacerbate your habit; you may even want to share the reasons why you're no longer hanging out with them.

Remember the comments made by Dr. Patricia in Chapter 1; the more she spoke with her colleagues about debt, the more she realized that they were as totally clueless as she had been. You may be in a similar position where you can help someone else with their personal finances.

Avoid Areas That Entice Spending

We each have certain weak spots for things when it comes to money and our spending habits. Whether this is online shopping through our favorite store or visiting the local mall and going on a spending spree, if you know what your trigger is for reckless behavior, make a change and find something to replace this habit. Even a good old rubber band around your wrist might work.

Try to put a rubber band around your wrist on your right hand. Whenever you're tempted to spend recklessly, pull the band back, and let it go so that it snaps against your wrist. Remove the band, and put it onto the left hand now. Continue following this process until you become conscious of the thought patterns that are leading you to this kind of spending.

Buy Second-Hand Instead of New

Rather than purchasing the latest model car, consider buying something that's second-hand, reliable, and in a good condition at a fraction of the price. According to finance expert Dave Ramsey, a new car depreciates in value by more than half its original worth within the first four years you own it. He compares this to throwing a $100 bill out of the window each week for four years.

There's a solution to this, however, and that's looking for a good-quality second-hand vehicle instead of paying the price tag for a new one.

Can You Survive with One Car?

You may want to consider whether you can get away with one car rather than two. This will depend on a number of different circumstances, such as the location where you and your family live.

You can test whether you can live with one vehicle before you actually sell one by parking one of them for a while and trying to carpool, cycle, walk, or make use of public transportation as a means of getting your costs down.

It's believed that you can save as much as $9,000 per year on operational expenses per vehicle that you get rid of. That's a huge amount of money that you can allocate towards debt repayments. Also, if the vehicle you sell is one you have an active loan for, you can immediately remove a car payment from your expenses.

Consolidate Your Debt

Debt consolidation is a means of paying everything off by financing another loan for the full amount of debt that you owe. While this can settle all of your debts in one go, you will be responsible for the new debt. Thus, be wary of going down the debt consolidation route, because you may not be able to afford the single new repayment plan.

The chances are that the payment term will be reduced, and depending on the size of the loan, it could be more than you have the capacity to repay in the term offered. On a short-term loan, the interest could also be much higher than your current debt is, although you will no longer have interest compounding.

Where this is a good idea is if your repayment amount is less than all of your current repayments at the moment. If you can continue paying this consolidated debt off at a higher rate every month (even by $100 more), then you will save on interest and be able to set aside the total amount much more quickly than if you paid it off in your negotiated term. This can save you hundreds or even thousands in interest.

Counsel with a Debt Specialist

It is always advisable to get in touch with someone who specializes in financial matters for sound advice. If you're ill, you're not going to drag yourself to a chef for medical advice; you're going to invest in yourself by visiting a specialist who has experience and has studied medicine.

Yet, when we find ourselves in a hole, we often ask everyone for advice besides those who are qualified to counsel us.

Do yourself a favor, and make contact with a debt counselor for a free consultation. There are so many companies and organizations out there that are prepared to offer free information and advice, so why not reach out and educate yourself?

Cut Your Budget

For the maximum benefit in trying to settle all your outstanding debts as quickly as possible, hack your current monthly budget as much as you possibly can. This will mean changing your lifestyle drastically and doing some things completely differently. Remember that this is only short-term. As you manage to claw your way out of your debt pit, you can begin adding certain items back into your monthly expenses (yet conservatively).

Focus on Largest Debts

When trying to flatten your debt as quickly as possible, the method that may work for you is taking on the largest debts with the highest interest rates and working aggressively at paying these debts off as soon as possible. This will then free up a substantial amount of money for the rest of your debt.

Monitor Spending Habits

Keep accurate records of your spending habits so you know where all your money is really going. This is similar to joining your colleagues each day as they eat out or order from fast food vendors. By cutting back on these spending habits daily, you will be astounded by how much money you are able to save.

Mortgage Refinancing

This is also something that should be considered almost as a last resort (along with debt consolidation). Depending on your current age, mortgage refinancing may take you well into your retirement years; and you really don't want to still be paying a major expense like a mortgage when you should be enjoying your glory days relaxing.

Only consider this if you know that you are planning on repaying this debt in a much shorter term than the one you negotiate with your financial institution.

Negotiate Interest

When negotiating directly with your creditors, try to get them to compromise on an interest freeze or waiving the interest completely. We've already discussed how creditors feel about having to pay excessive commissions to collection agencies or losing out completely and only getting pennies on the dollar. Due to this, they should be open to these negotiations.

Pay Extra

In the short term, you should pay more than you owe on each of your debts. An extra $50 to $100 can make a world of a difference in reducing interest rates and eating into the initial debt amount, helping you pay off your debts in record time.

Spend Less

We've discussed working with a budget when it comes to all your shopping needs. However, even when you have a budget and plan in place, try to spend less than what you've planned. Whatever you manage to save can either be added to a specific fund for a couple of months, and then a lump sum payment can be made toward one of your debts, or you can divide this amount up over each of your accounts to help you pay off your debts more quickly.

Store Foods

Whenever you come across really excellent prices and you have the money in your budget, stock up on sale items. Consider doing this with non-perishable items such as tinned foods. If there are other items that can be frozen over time, then add these to your shopping list, as well.

After you do this over several months, there will come a time where you actually have enough groceries at your disposal that you only need to buy perishable products such as bread and milk, fresh fruit, and vegetables for the month's purchases.

Only look at doing this whenever there are exceptionally good prices and you've done your homework and checked prices at other stores. Also, make sure you are 100% certain that you've come across a true bargain. Even adding one bargain per month can quickly add up so that you save almost a month's worth of grocery costs.

Common Mistakes

There are a number of common mistakes that people make when they're trying to get out of debt. Instead of making their lives simpler by getting out from under all the debt that's swallowing them whole, they fall into these common traps:

Apply for Debt Relief

The mistake that's often made when applying for debt relief is not understanding the process behind relief and rehabilitation. This is not going to get you out of the hole any time soon. You need to be prepared to be patient as this process will keep you tied up for between three and five years. In addition to this, you are now paying compounded interest because the debt relief organization also takes their cut monthly. This means that what you're paying them is NOT what's being paid over to your creditors (which is not great news at all).

Avoid making this mistake by asking the debt relief organization as many questions as possible. If you choose to go down this avenue, please do so with both eyes open and be fully educated about the entire process.

Closing Accounts

Many people make the common mistake of closing out their accounts the moment their debt is settled. By all means, cut up your cards so you know that you cannot run up the account again. However, it's important to leave the account open. Remember that your credit score will be influenced by your actual ability to get credit. This won't be possible if you've closed your accounts.

Debt Is Not Important

Ignorance is bliss for those who don't recognize that they have a debt problem or try to bury their heads in the sand. By ignoring creditors—their letters of demand, and phone calls—you are actually making the situation much worse for yourself. The debt is not magically going to go away (no matter how hard we wish it would).

Hiding from your problems is not a solution. Facing up to the cold hard truth and taking responsibility for the financial situation you're in is within your hands. It's your responsibility to make things right.

Impractical Budgeting

Budgeting incorrectly (whether you're way over or way under) is not a solution to your financial woes. The only way that you can get accurate figures is by following the steps we laid out for you in Chapter 3 to plan a budget.

You must know what your income and expenditure are for your budget to be anywhere near accurate. The only way to get this information is by tracking your spending on your bank statements over a three-month period.

Lack of Emergency Fund

We've already recommended that before you start any of your repayments, you should find $1,000 to set aside as an emergency fund. This is specifically there for any emergency situation that you may find yourself in.

Refuse to Change

Accept that to save enough money to pay your debts, you need to alter the way you view and spend money. Your entire relationship with it needs to be different. This means brown-bagging lunches and enjoying your breakfast and morning cup of coffee at home, rather than stopping at Starbucks on your way to the office.

Too Tough to Ask for Help

Pretending that you don't need help or that you know everything is not a wise move at all. Unless you are a financial expert, you can never get enough advice from those who know what they are doing. Don't be too proud or stubborn to ask for assistance.

Trying to Do Too Much

Making the mistake of trying to pay off too many debts too quickly can easily lead to your own undoing. There's a time and season for each of your debts, and while you may wish that they would all go away at the wave of a wand, you could end up in financial trouble where you don't have enough money for your actual living expenses for the month. Instead, practice some restraint and patience in settling your debts.

Verifying Credit

Do yourself a favor on a regular basis and check your current credit score via Experian or a similar source. You are entitled to one free credit check per year for yourself. Go through this document carefully to ensure that the information contained therein is correct. Debt that has already been settled should be removed. You may even discover that you have debt that's incorrectly allocated against your name.

It's worth verifying your current credit status every few months. Search for those credit bureaus that offer this service in your state or country, and stagger your requests for these reports every couple of months so you can monitor the movement as you pay off your creditors.

What's Your Motivation?

Remember your motivation. There's no easy way to financial freedom other than the tried and tested slog. Make as many financial sacrifices as you can and stay motivated throughout the process. This journey will certainly have highs and lows. It's easy to be motivated when things are going well and you can physically see the debt disappearing before your eyes. However, how do you keep motivated when things are taking longer than expected?

When you feel as though you're hitting a brick, please know that this is part of the process. Some of your larger debts can take years to get rid of, and while you may be motivated initially, that feeling can soon turn to frustration and anxiety if you lose sight of what you're actually doing it all for.

This is especially true if you're working through a debt collection agency and you know that they're taking this chunk of change from whatever you're paying them; all the while, your principal debt is hardly seeing any of your contribution towards chipping away at the capital amount.

You will certainly experience rough times, so you need to find ways to push through the pain to make it worthwhile for yourself. This way, you can resist the urge to simply throw in the towel and give up.

Some secrets for staying motivated are outlined below.

Draw Up Your Plan

Be sure that you have all the information captured regarding your plan to get out of debt and stay that way. It's ideal to have this information outlined on an Excel spreadsheet, along with all your other financial information.

Find Someone to Be Accountable To

Being accountable to someone keeps you motivated toward achievement because you will need to report back to them on your progress. If you become demotivated, they are there to pull you back on track and help pump you up again. Having someone to share this journey with is important.

Stay Informed

Do whatever it takes to stay updated on all the latest information by following debt professional blogs and websites. You can find these by searching the internet or scouring YouTube for debt specialists.

You can also search for podcasts that you can listen to in order to keep up with the latest trends. Reading some of these blogs can help keep you motivated, especially when you feel you're heading toward a slump.

Remind Yourself of Your Motivation

Think about all the major reasons you're getting out of debt, and write all of these points in a journal. You can refer back to it whenever you happen to be feeling down.

Reward Yourself

Set up a reward system for yourself where you allow yourself a specific treat that's within a reasonable price range (something like a latte at your favorite coffee shop). You can allocate other rewards as you manage to pay off an account, once again within reason. The main idea is that you celebrate the progress that you're making toward becoming totally debt-free without adopting bad spending habits again.

Set a Date

As you begin to see things happen as you manage to settle one account after another, set a due date for when you'd like to be completely debt-free. This date should be placed somewhere that you can see it each and every day.

Remember the push and pull of your debt-free motivation—wanting to avoid debt is the push side of things, while the pull is the positive life you'll be able to enjoy once you are completely debt-free.

Chapter 6:

Rebuild Your Credit

"A good financial plan is a road map that shows us exactly how the choices we make today will affect our future." ~ *Alexa von Tobel*

By now, you are well on your way toward getting out of debt, and you should be extremely proud of yourself for making it this far. The next goal in your journey toward financial freedom is rebuilding your credit one step at a time. Learning how your credit score works and is calculated is the first thing that you need to do to begin to rebuild.

How to Rebuild Your Credit

Step 1: Obtain a Copy of Your Credit Score

We have already recommended that you find out who you can make contact with to obtain updated credit score information on a regular basis. You are entitled to a free credit report on yourself every twelve months. Studying this document will tell you what is having the greatest impact on your credit score. If you are making regular payments or have managed to settle some of your outstanding debt, remember to give the credit bureaus time to alter their records accordingly. This may take a while.

In the event that you're hoping to be able to use this document, you can always provide a copy of your settlement documents to the person who is doing the credit check. They will then be able to manually ignore the debt that appears on your report. Your actual credit score is generated electronically and is dependent on two factors and two factors only, which are detailed below.

How Much Money You Have at Your Disposal

Can you now understand why we mentioned earlier that you most certainly should not close off any accounts that are currently "paid-up"? They will still reflect that you have an account with them and how much actual credit you have with each financial institution or retail institution. Up to 70% of your credit rating is depending on this score.

Your Repayment History

How quickly and accurately you repay your debt adds to the above percentage. If you are making minimum monthly payments on time, and you haven't defaulted, your score will be good.

Step 2: Pay on Time All the Time

As much as you can, make sure that you're able to honor your financial commitments by paying the minimum amount due. If you settle an account for less than the principal amount, it will negatively influence your credit score. This habit of repayment should be applied to all of your accounts and not just to credit cards and financial institutions. Should you default on a payment or be late paying for something, catch up as soon as possible.

Did you know that any late payments show up as negatives on your credit score for seven years? However, obviously, as time passes, the older debts are not as important as those that are current.

Experian Boost

You can influence your credit score positively if you pay your utility bills and cell phone bill on time by making use of Experian Boost, which can be found on the Experian website.

When working with your credit report, check for discrepancies, and deal with them immediately. You may discover that there are various accounts listed on your credit report that have either been paid in full and should be removed or that don't belong to you at all. This is probably one of the most damaging situations. Make contact with the agency to verify, and be certain that corrective action is taken as a matter of urgency.

Step 3: Working With Credit Cards

Keep Credit Card Debt Balances to a Minimum

It's wise to pay off all outstanding debt as quickly as possible and leave small amounts due on your credit card and/or revolving credit account. The reason for this is that this is directly linked to your credit utilization ratios. This is calculated by your current credit balance divided by your total available credit. This would produce what is known as your credit utilization ratio.

This rate is usually optimum when it's around 30% or lower. You can achieve this ratio by keeping your credit card or revolving credit debts low and paid on time.

Retail Credit Cards

Don't sign up for those retail credit cards so you can flash them around. The truth is that these do nothing to influence your credit rating positively. They can, however, cause you damage if you're unable to pay them, you default, or you pay them less than what is owed. This is just another trick to get you further into the debt pit and back into that vicious cycle of overspending.

Leave Paid-Up Credit Cards Alone

By closing out your paid-up credit cards, you increase your credit score because it reflects that you don't have any credit available—or, it can impact your credit utilization ratios negatively rather than positively. If you can imagine that you still owe the same amount on a card that's open, but all your others are now closed (and your credit limit on the card is less also), it stands to reason that once you start to crunch the numbers, you're only doing it against one card versus several.

Applying for Too Many Accounts

This will often raise red flags with the various credit bureaus. If you are planning on applying for a number of different credit options, be sure to stagger them over a period of time. Too many credit checks all happening at the same time can look suspicious. This type of check is known as a hard inquiry and remains on your credit score for up to two years.

Step 4: Rebuilding Your Credit Score

I often get asked how long it takes to rebuild a credit score that's taken a couple of knocks because of bad debt, delinquency in paying off accounts, or good old ostrich syndrome (burying your head in the sand and hoping for the best). Unfortunately, the answer to this question is probably not the one that you want to hear.

There's no quick fix to repairing a bad credit score other than paying off your debts and submitting the "paid-up" letters to the credit bureaus.

Once your debt has been repaid, if you change your spending habits and pay regularly—and you avoid delinquency and other bad debts—then all you can do is wait.

Here's the reality of how long each of these remains under your name with the credit bureau:

- Delinquent accounts: Seven years

- Public records: Seven to ten years, depending on whether you've filed for bankruptcy or not

- All inquiries: Remain on your report for a two-year period

There's no quick fix for rebuilding your credit score; you must simply wait it out. Should you happen to open new accounts, be sure to pay them on time so that you don't go back into any negative delinquency reports.

Step 5: Change Credit Behavior

Most people who are sitting with a bad credit score got there because they slipped into some bad habits as far as debt was concerned. One of the easiest ways to get out of this jam is by changing each of these bad habits regarding credit and deciding to keep all of your accounts current. That means paying all your bills on time all the time, without skipping any of them or allowing your accounts to fall back into that pit.

It's all about being honest and owning the fact that you are responsible for your current debt situation.

Get Out of Debt ASAP!

If you're still sitting with bad debt or delinquent accounts, work tirelessly to get them paid off as a matter of urgency. The seven years we spoke of earlier on only starts counting down once all of your debts are settled. We've covered a lot of ideas in earlier chapters regarding ways you can cut back and tackle each of these outstanding accounts as aggressively as possible. Find the smallest debt on your credit listing, and move mountains to get rid of it.

How to Rebuild After a Collection

Before you even start working on this, you need to understand what this means and how it affects your credit report. When referring to delinquencies on your credit report, these are accounts that are in arrears for months because the bills just haven't been paid. This impacts 35% of your actual credit score, which is not very good news at all.

As long as you're sitting with one or both these types of charges on your credit score, you will probably keep on being declined for any form of credit whatsoever. This could even be for silly things like cell phone contracts, not to mention rental agreements and so forth. The good news is that you can get rid of this.

Incorrect Charges

We've discussed the importance of ensuring the accuracy of your credit report and disputing any listings that don't belong to you. What we haven't done is told you how to do this. Be sure that all of your communications regarding the dispute are done in writing. There should be one set of documents (letter of dispute) that goes to the credit bureau and another set that goes directly to the so-called creditor.

What's important to note is that the credit bureau has 45 days to investigate the matter and get back to you. By the end of this period, your credit report should be either updated or you should receive a written communication back from them stating why it is not going to be updated.

Pay Off Your Accounts

Get to a zero balance as quickly as you can, and keep it there. Provide the credit bureau with a copy of all "paid-up" letters so they can attach these to your credit report. When applying for new credit, be sure to have all of this documentation handy as proof that these amounts have, in fact, been paid and that you are sitting with a zero balance on these accounts.

There's an option called a "pay for delete" letter where you can offer to settle an account in exchange for the debt to be expunged from your credit record. In the event that the creditor agrees to this, get them to send you a signed proof of their agreement to do so before paying them anything.

Settling

This is also not the greatest of options to consider, because settling indicates that you have come to an arrangement regarding the amount that you're willing or able to pay. It indicates that there was a trade-off. This may potentially hurt you more than it will help you. If it's the only way you can afford to repay the outstanding amount, then you may not have any other choice in the matter.

Remember, the duration for any debt on your credit report is seven years. If you find that this seven-year term is fast approaching its end, it may be worth it to just leave it and let it drop off on its own.

Rebuilding

This is much the same as rebuilding normal credit. Try to keep at least one credit card going where you put through some minor charges each month, and allow these to be paid by debit card so they're taken off of your account automatically each month. Be sure that any loan accounts are paid in full and on time. This way, you can build a positive track record showing you are reliable and know how to work with your money.

There are ways of opening secured credit cards where you need a credit balance in the account at all times. You will be able to use this as a credit card as long as you keep up with each of the payments each month.

Removing Default Information

Another way of trying to get default payment information removed is by requesting the party who was dealing with the outstanding account to kindly remove the delinquency from your credit score as a "goodwill gesture". This is similar to a "pay for delete" option, but the creditor doesn't have to do you any favors. Here, you would be appealing to them on a personal level by being honest and explaining why you were in the situation you were in.

A word of caution when going this route—you are appealing to someone's human nature, and by law, they don't have to do anything for you. You may just have some luck on your side that they feel sorry for you and agree to work with you rather than against you.

How to Rebuild Credit Fast

Some individuals may not be content with waiting it out or may be antsy to restore their credit rating as soon as possible. The good news is that each of the major credit bureaus update their information every month. That means that you have a 30-day window each month to improve your credit rating.

The downside of having a bad credit rating is that it negatively impacts your ability to secure credit from just about anyone. Vehicle finance houses are occasionally prepared to help you out, as well as mortgage lenders, but your penalties or interest rates on this credit are going to be sky-high. The only way to do anything about it is by digging your way out of the hole and trying to fix your credit report yourself.

Don't fall for companies who make empty promises saying they will do it on your behalf. Sure, there are some that can be reliable, but when you really think about it, they don't have the same drive and passion to get this handled as quickly and painlessly as possible; it's not their name that's being pulled through the mud, but yours.

Once again, before starting this process, you need to get as many free credit reports as you can while trying to avoid the scammers out there. Some companies/organizations promising free credit reports are actually trying to get you to pay for their product. The top three to consider using are Experian, Equifax, and TransUnion. These are totally free, and you may request one free credit report from each of them annually.

Here are our top tips on how to get out of the hole after bankruptcy.

After Bankruptcy

Believe it or not, many lenders out there consider those coming back after bankruptcy to be low-risk, purely because they cannot file for bankruptcy again for another eight years. If this is the situation you find yourself in, be sure to pay everything that you owe as quickly as possible. Keep your payments happening on time, and try to pay more than the minimum balance. That way, you are likely to save yourself money in unnecessary interest, and you can show your creditors that you have now learned to become more responsible with your finances.

It's also important that you learn how to manage your money as best you can without having to rely on loans too quickly. This is not always going to be easy, but living frugally can often be the answer for someone who is learning to start again.

Authorized User on Someone's Account

If you know of someone who has a good credit score and doesn't abuse their credit card(s), you could ask them whether you can become an authorized user on their account. This will reflect on your own credit rating and not theirs. You would need to treat this as any new credit account attached to your credit rating.

Use this card for smaller purchases, and make regular minimum payments to keep the card current. Remember that someone is trusting you with their credit rating as well, so don't disappoint them by running up huge debts that you can't afford to pay back.

Credit Utilization Score

Concentrate on your credit utilization ratio by paying off most of your debts on credit cards, and try to erase any large credit card debt completely (without closing out accounts). It's recommended that you look to keep the debt that you owe on credit cards between 10 and 30% of your total credit limit(s).

Increase Your Limit

Another solution to the same problem could be requesting for some of the limits on your cards to be increased. The obvious thing would be to ensure that if this is granted, you don't take advantage of the additional credit and max the card out.

Make Two Payments

Another way of rebuilding your credit faster is by making two payments on your credit card each month. If you can manage to pay close to the time when the statement is issued and again by the due date, it will reflect on the major credit bureaus in your region.

Multiple Credit Streams

Rather than settling just for credit cards, mix it up a little so you have a variety of credit that you're using. When looking at big-ticket items like a television or funds to pay for a medical procedure, consider applying for a personal loan that is short-term. This will boost your credit score by indicating that no matter the type of credit you currently have, you will manage it like a pro, making sure that it's paid-up in a responsible manner.

Open Another Account

This will increase how much credit you have access to, and it can also increase your credit utilization score. This is good news for you. Just remember to keep this account low by making payments on it often. Try to keep a very small balance on this account by making small purchases and paying for them each month.

Pay on Time, Every Time

If 35% of your overall score is linked to your repayment history, then you will understand why it's so important to pay your accounts as they are due. Set reminders for yourself when they are due if you struggle to remember when specific accounts need to be paid; or, at the time of negotiation, arrange that all payments go off within the same week as one another. That way, you will know that during the last week of the month or the first week of the month, all your debt needs to be paid.

Another way of dealing with this is to schedule auto-pay facilities. Then you know that they will be paid each month like clockwork, without you having to worry about remembering dates.

Speak to Collection Agencies

Most collection agencies bought your debt for a fraction of what it is really worth and may be willing to negotiate a settlement with you. Try to enter into negotiations with them to find out whether they would be willing to write off some of the debt and settle for a smaller amount. Always be certain that you can afford to pay them this amount of money.

If you have been saving for a few months, this may be an ideal time to use this money to settle slightly larger accounts without putting too much additional strain on your budget. Because they bought your debt for a fraction of what it is worth, they may be willing to settle with you. After all, receiving some payment on the debt is better than getting nothing at all.

Work Through Credit Reports Thoroughly

Go through each of your credit reports with a fine-tooth comb, and correct any discrepancies. It's important that you have sufficient evidentiary proof to provide the credit bureaus rather than just calling them to tell them that their report is wrong. Remember, we've already discussed that they have a 45-day window in which to investigate; they will either clear your credit history or come back to you with sufficient proof that their information is correct.

Be sure that any and all communication is done in writing. You need a proper paper trail to fix your current credit score. This will also lead to possibly being able to remove paid-up accounts, once again by submitting paid-up documents proving that accounts are now sitting with a zero balance. This can be an important step in the process, because not every collection agency will automatically submit or send paid-up information through to the credit bureaus.

There's simply no quick fix for getting out of debt and fixing your credit score with credit bureaus. It takes time for any and all debts to work through the system. Along with this time, it's going to take patience on your part. Be prepared to wait it out once you've done everything that you can to resolve your debts.

Stop Overspending

One of the easiest ways to bring debt down on your credit report is to curb those spending habits monthly. Avoid spending more than you make each month. This includes making a plan to pay more than the minimum amount due on each of your credit cards monthly. If you can only manage one at a time, then choose the lowest one, pay it off, move onto the next one, and so forth, using Dave Ramsey's snowball method.

Chapter 7:

Stay Out

"A big part of financial freedom is having your heart and mind free from worry about the what-ifs of life." ~ *Suze Orman*

Now that you're successfully out of the debt pit and are slowly in the process of rebuilding your credit, it's time to look at implementing long-term strategies and habits that will keep you from falling back into the same debt pit again.

In this chapter, we are going to discover how you can stay out of debt while forming good money habits that will sustain you throughout your life.

How to Stay Out of Debt

It may have taken you many months of making large personal sacrifices to be able to make the final payment on your accounts, and it most likely feels amazing. You should be proud of what you have been able to accomplish in meeting these financial goals. At this point, it probably even feels like it has been an eternity since you resolved your debt. It has undoubtedly taken discipline and saving every dime you could possibly lay your hands on to get here.

The big question now is how do you manage to stay out of debt moving forward? You know how much it has taken for you to get to this point, and the last thing you want to do is relive this same process again. Well, congratulations. You have actually taken the first step to staying out of debt—by deciding you never want to be caught in this situation again.

This is often easier said than done because life happens—emergencies happen where we need more than we have available. However, there are a couple of simple rules you can follow to help you stay out of as much debt as possible, which are detailed below.

Avoid Proportionate Increases

Try to avoid increasing your monthly budget directly in line with an income increase. This is not always possible as the cost of living increases substantially each year, and your increase may hardly even cover your basic needs. In the event that it is a possibility for you, however, add this into your savings account rather than being tempted to increase your living expenses. If you only need a portion of your increase to be allocated toward your living expenses, then split it accordingly, and save, save, save!

Choose a Debit Card

You can do as much with a debit card as you can with a credit card, with the exception of running up debt. This is a good thing. All your purchases can only happen if you're sitting with a positive balance in your account. If you don't have cash in your account, you will be forced to go without, which may be a bit of an inconvenience at the time.

However, this inconvenience is short-lived compared with facing a credit card charge at the end of the month for the "instant gratification" attitude. The bonus of choosing this option is that you never have to worry about facing another shock credit card bill ever again. The total peace of mind at the end of the day is worth its weight in gold.

Another upside of using debit cards is that there are usually rewards attached to them that credit cards don't always offer. More retail and consumer outlets are offering loyalty reward programs which also offer discounts on the spot, making this even more attractive. Even financial institutions are prepared to reward you if you remain within your agreed monthly balances.

Choose to Live Frugally

Living a frugal life means you are cautious and conservative when it comes to money management and living. You can manage your resources effectively and can make do with what you have. In the old days, they may have referred to someone living a frugal life as a thrifty individual.

Frugality is rapidly becoming fashionable. This means you need to make better, wiser decisions in all aspects of your life involving money and spending. One way individuals are doing this is by living according to a strict budget. This involves actual physical work and planning on your part before racing off to the store and adding whatever you would like into your grocery cart. It means working from a shopping list and being disciplined enough to stick within your budget.

To get to this point, you may need to track your current spending habits (down to the last penny) for up to three months. Once you have all of this information, you can begin crossing items off of your list that you know you can actually do without.

Some ideas that come to mind are magazine subscriptions that you seldom use. Cancel them, even if there is a small cancellation fee, as this is better than throwing good money away each month that you are not utilizing. Are you a compulsive shopper at one particular store? Do you often find yourself going into this store just to "browse", and then you leave the store having spent $200? You will definitely notice this once you start going through your spending history.

Be brutally honest with yourself. Did you really need anything that you bought from your favorite store, or were you shopping on impulse? Remember how we spoke about buyer's remorse at the beginning of this book? This remorse is not only limited to large expenses. Buyer's remorse can also kick in the moment we spend money unnecessarily on things we know we don't need.

Choosing to live a frugal life means you can still maintain your lifestyle, but instead of impulse shopping, you should be more selective about what you are spending your hard-earned dollars on. Go back over your spending habits, and decide what you can live without and what needs to stay on your list.

Being frugal does not mean avoiding spending altogether; it means being wiser about your spending choices and making lifestyle changes that are going to prove to be wiser. It may surprise you how much money you can save by making some minor lifestyle changes.

Continue Setting Financial Goals

Your main financial goals initially might have been to get out of financial debt to enjoy a life that was debt-free. Having achieved this goal doesn't mean that you should now kick back and let things happen again. Rather, it provides you with the brilliant opportunity of beginning to set some new financial goals. Whether this is saving to buy that secondhand car or saving toward a fabulous family vacation, set your goal by stipulating the exact amount you would like to save and by when.

Also, don't merely help yourself to the funds you have sitting in your savings. These funds are for emergencies only. Setting financial goals you can clearly visualize won't only help you stay out of debt, but they can also help you be way more responsible in your spending habits.

Find a Side Hustle

This could be anything from pet care, photography, writing, or signing up on several freelance sites to bid for work. There is no such thing as a "get rich quick" scheme, and many of these side hustles are going to take up a lot of your free time, if not all of it. Be prepared for this as the payoffs can be worth it.

As far as freelancing goes, some of the sites you can utilize are free, while others request a small donation (fee) for you to be able to pitch for work. Some of these sites include Upwork, Craigslist, Fiver, and Freelancer.

As an example, you may be excellent with SEO or developing websites, so put yourself out there and see what you can pick up as extra work. This is especially relevant when you are trying to get out of debt. Who knows, your side hustle could prove to be so profitable that you decide to do it full-time.

Keep Monitoring Your Credit Score

Just as you tried to get your credit score as high as you possibly could while paying off your debt, it is important to keep your credit score at an optimum level. We have discussed this at length. The key takeaway from this is that you can get benefits from most of your accounts once you have managed to restore your credit score. Part of this maintenance is ensuring that you avoid running up any new debt because you make a point of paying whatever you owe at the end of each month.

Know Your Limits

Make it your responsibility to find out as much as you can about the various fees and additional charges you are paying on each of your accounts. Become finance savvy rather than remaining in ignorance when it comes to your finances. Accountability, especially surrounding financial education, is your responsibility.

One of the first places you can begin is by setting up an appointment with your personal banker or financial advisor. Ask them to provide you with all the information regarding where charges come in on your account(s). This could be anything from your current checking account to credit and loan accounts.

There are many accounts that allow you to repay your entire outstanding balance in six months with a zero-interest rate. These are the credit cards that you want to be working with, as long as you are disciplined enough to be able to repay outstanding charges within the stipulated six-month period. The most obvious benefit is that interest charges are waived on these accounts.

Areas that carry charges include bank transfers and other transactions on your account. Be sure that you understand exactly what each of these charges is and how they are incurred.

A bank might claim their charges are limited to a couple of dollars monthly, yet when you study your bank statements more closely, you may discover you are being charged a certain percentage per transaction over and above what your bank charges are.

When these charges are unrealistic, it may be time for you to shop around for a better financial institution where there are no hidden costs attached to your account.

Limit Credit Card Spending

If you must have a credit card, set yourself a monthly limit as to what you can spend. Once you've reached this particular amount, ask a trusted family member to lock your card away safely until the debt has been paid, and you can then press the reset button on your card spending habits. Be sure to keep this figure low enough that you know you can meet these costs every month.

Being in possession of your card can always open you up to temptation. Be sure that you can avoid these temptations, and curb your spending habits to match your self-imposed credit limitations.

Not All Savings Accounts Are Equal

When it comes to savings accounts, it pays to find ones that are going to give you the highest yields or return on your investment. Many of these require a minimum deposit and could also be fixed for a particular term. This is a good thing as it means you cannot simply draw your savings from your account on a whim.

Ensuring your savings have some form of fixed term attached to them is a wise decision. This will force you to seriously consider whether you really need whatever you wanted the funds for.

Shop around for the bank that is going to give you the highest returns in interest. These are often referred to as "high yield savings accounts". In many instances, they pay out up to 20 times more than conventional savings accounts.

Pay Cash

We all know how convenient it is to swipe using a credit card or bank card rather than carrying cash around with you, but this could be a bit of a fine line on a double-edged sword. Every time you are swiping your card, you are incurring service fees and bank charges. Withdrawing cash attracts charges which vary depending on where you are pulling it from. So, your dilemma is this: do you incur bank charges and draw $200 from your account because you are not sure how much money you are going to need, or do you run the risk of running short on money because you know that you have your card as a back-up?

Personally, I hate carrying cash around with me for several reasons. I know if I have $20 or $200 in my wallet, I will find something to spend it on (this is where frivolous spending comes in). On the other hand, if I am swiping my card and I know I have no cash on me, I cannot overspend.

If you are disciplined enough with your spending habits, then try to use cash rather than simply swiping. If you are used to your groceries costing you $120, then withdrawing $150 is going to cover your groceries and the small amount left is not going to make a major dent in your budget.

When you use cash or a debit card instead of a credit card, it can help you budget more carefully as you will always know exactly what your balance is at any given time.

Reconsider Your Housing Costs

A study conducted by Harvard University and the Joint Center for Housing Studies in 2016 revealed that many Americans were classified as being "severely cost-burdened" when it came to their monthly housing costs. It further showed that most were paying more than half their monthly take-home pay on housing costs (Joint Center for Housing Studies, 2016). In the event of this happening, individuals were forced to make other important sacrifices in the form of saving toward their retirement or paying for a healthcare plan.

Because living costs are so high, there is a greater risk of these individuals falling behind in debt. If you find that this is your present situation, then it may be time to start looking for cheaper accommodation elsewhere, even if it is a short-term solution for you to be able to get back on your feet.

There may be a number of reasons for falling into this category. Perhaps you or your spouse have been laid off, or you have had your work hours cut back which directly impacts your earnings. The moment you can confirm that you are spending more than half of your combined income on housing, it is time to face reality and consider what your options are.

Set Aside Savings First

Very few Americans have any form of savings account(s) in place, let alone an emergency fund. Calculate what you can set aside each month, and put this into a savings account first thing. Ideally, you should have anywhere between three and six months' worth of take-home pay as a buffer, emergency fund. Depending on the type of job you are working, this amount may need to increase to an annual salary.

Please understand that being able to save this kind of money is not going to happen overnight. That is, unless you are disciplined and serious enough to be able to get rid of absolutely anything and everything that you no longer need or plan to use again in the future. Make this a regular monthly habit.

The secret to building this fund faster is by making use of any additional income that you were not expecting and setting aside this money as well. Examples of this kind of income could be tax refunds, bonus payouts, or financial windfalls such as an inheritance or investment dividends. As each of these is paid out, rather than spending the funds frivolously on things you do not need and you know you are going to regret, put this money to good use by saving it.

You never know what might happen to you and/or a member of your family where this additional income may be necessary. Common things that go wrong are large household repairs that fall outside of warranty, auto repairs, and long-term medical costs that are outside of your insurance limit.

Did you know that the average American will spend $279,002 on interest rates alone throughout the average lifetime?

Cut Off Online Ordering

Being in the habit of shopping online can be a form of addiction, especially if you are on the store's mailing list. Marketing specialists are specifically trained to sell you stuff, and there are some very fancy algorithms that are applied which can predict your specific buying patterns.

In simple terms, they know exactly what you want before you do. They take your location, age, average income, hobbies into account. Most importantly, they view your browsing history. That's right, all the different sites that you visit determine what news you get in your inbox every day, and this is also a keen predictor of what your personal tastes are likely to be.

Shopping online may be a quick and easy fix when you are looking for something in particular, and you really do not have the time to drive around searching for that item. And it's true that this can save you a lot of money in gas, and it can save you loads of time.

Where online shopping becomes a problem is when you find yourself bored, so hop online and browse your favorite stores. You might add items to your cart shamelessly without really reading product reviews to find out whether other customers were satisfied with their purchase or not.

I am not a huge fan of online shopping myself, and generally only consider it when I know that I have done my homework and the price is an absolute bargain. I usually read through as many product reviews as possible, check out the overall product rating, and then review prices for the same product through conventional stores. If the item is still cheaper online, I may concede and purchase that way, although it always leaves my stomach in knots until the item arrives in good condition.

A short while ago, I went on the hearsay of an acquaintance of mine and when the price seemed too good to be true, I literally jumped at the chance, committed to making the purchase. Then, I waited. By the time the item finally arrived, I was totally disappointed. It was definitely not what I had envisioned, and that buyer's remorse hit home immediately. To date, I have used the item only once, and because it is now second-hand, I will need to settle for whatever somebody offers me for it.

Stop being sucked into all the major hype that is created as part of the convenience of online shopping. Even with trusted sites like Amazon and Etsy, if you are not really disciplined enough to stick within a budget, you could find yourself running up hefty amounts that will be billed back to your credit card.

Don't Be Too Afraid to Talk About Finances

What is the big secret surrounding your finances? So many individuals in committed relationships and even married couples have issues communicating openly with each other about finances. This should be one of the things that are at the top of your list of points to talk about long before you either move in together or tie the knot. You need to know what you are signing up for and whether you will be in a position to afford the things that you really want out of life. Otherwise, you will be looking down the barrel of a gun for the first few years of marriage trying to get out of debt.

There should be no secrets when it comes down to committed relationships. Each party is probably going to come with their own baggage of some sort, but you must be able to work through this together to devise a workable solution. Once you reach an amicable agreement, both parties should be prepared to do whatever it takes to see it through to the end.

You may find that if you have an excessive amount of debts that need to be settled. Perhaps due to this, your partner has become a bit skittish or iffy about sharing the responsibility of helping you get out of the hole that you are in. I can promise you that when you work together to reach financial goals, it will strengthen your relationship more than you could ever imagine.

What starts off as something that is really tough will see you both coming out the other side much stronger as individuals, and your relationship will be able to withstand almost anything afterward.

Download a Budgeting App

With the advancements in technology today, why not make use of a budgeting app that can assist you in managing your finances? There are several apps that are currently available that have been designed specifically to meet your needs as an individual.

There are apps for saving, monthly budgeting, managing your monthly bills, and everything in between. You can even complete a detailed income and expenditure plan on some of them. This certainly can make working with your finances extremely user-friendly and, dare I say, fun.

Enjoy Your Cup of Coffee at Home

When it comes to keeping your expenses in the black once you have worked so hard to get out of debt, one of the sacrifices you made was to give up stopping at Starbucks for your early morning coffee. Stick to the habit of drinking your coffee at home. If you have a lengthy commute and you are used to enjoying a coffee on the way, get yourself a thermos mug that you can fill at home and at the office before leaving so your sacrifice is minimal.

Admittedly, your options at home may be a bit limited initially depending on what you are used to ordering. However, it is pretty easy to make a mean mocha java at home. Be sure to buy different blends from the store during your monthly shop. Your pocket will thank you for it every single month.

This is not to say that you should never stop and enjoy your favorite brew at Starbucks ever again, but it should be a reward or a special treat rather than a daily habit.

Prioritize Credit Card Debt

You may be out of the hole when it comes to your credit card debt. It could have taken your blood, sweat, and loads of tears to bring it down to a point where the minimum balance is manageable. To avoid ending up in exactly the same situation all over again, be sure to pay the minimum amount outstanding each and every month. Next to your savings, these two payments should be prioritized as being the most important. Not only will this keep your current credit rating from being negatively affected, but it will also prove that you are now rehabilitated and can be trusted to manage your finances effectively.

Be aware, though, that all the other financial institutions may begin phoning you to offer you credit cards or various loan options. Do not get sucked back into this quagmire of debt once more. We have already explained the system to you; the banks and the government are there to ensure that you remain as dependent on debt as possible. This is how the financial institutions make their money—by keeping you stuck as much as they possibly can.

The more your boat is sinking in debt, the more they are racking in the interest. Plug the leak in your boat, and remove the water that made it through. Do not settle for this type of lifestyle anymore. You managed to see your way through it, and it might have taken you a number of years to see the light at the end of the tunnel.

Whatever you do, avoid climbing back into the hole.

Redeem Rewards

Loyalty and reward cards or points are often attached to your financial expenses each month. This could be anything from discount offers through specific partners to a cash-back reward system. Retail outlets also have various loyalty and reward programs. Some are instantaneous, while others work on a coupon system.

Earlier, we discussed collecting coupons as a way to help you trim your living expenses and cut your budget to the bone. Remember to redeem these points. Carry your loyalty cards around with you, and apply for cards for your spouse or partner so no matter who is shopping, you can still reap the rewards.

Look out for specials in stores close to your home. If you have a small family and specials are available as bulk deals, find family members or friends who are prepared to share in some of the costs with you. Be sure to only buy those items that you are going to use. This goes for all specials that you add to your groceries.

Only spend money on what you would normally eat. Remember to check prices between your local stores; you may discover that there is a substantial discount available on certain items in the same store. Yes, this may mean stopping at more than one store, but being able to save $50 on only a few grocery items is worth it.

Once again, swipe loyalty cards. Some of these cards offer immediate rewards, while others accumulate for up to twelve months. This could be a reasonable reward to spend on something special.

Reduce Your Time Spent Shopping

Rather than wandering up and down aisles in shops, write out your grocery list for at least a week or two. People often find that they have forgotten something the moment they pull into the driveway. Thus, they might end up making several trips back and forth to supermarkets on the same day or within a couple of days.

There is a solution to all the unnecessary driving back and forth to the store. Simply write out a comprehensive shopping list that you know will last you for at least a week or so. This will not only save you gas, but it will save wear and tear on your car and the frustration of discovering that you do not have all the ingredients you need to make one of your favorite dishes.

Working from a shopping list makes your trip a breeze as you do not need to guess which brands you want as you will already know this. Your list will ensure that you remember to get everything you need, and it will curb your spending on non-essential items. This will not only reduce the amount of time spent shopping, but it should have a positive effect on your budget as well.

Request Credit Alerts

A nifty add-on that you can request from your credit card company or financial institution is a notification when you are planning on making a hasty purchasing decision. Set your daily budget limit to a responsible amount. This will result in the credit card company making contact with you or sending you a text message to verify whether you are certain that you really want to make the purchase. They can also notify you once you are close to reaching your credit limit.

Putting these notifications in place can prevent you from impulse buying, and they might even make you consider whether you really need the item you are intending to purchase. This can save you a substantial amount of money and prevent buyer's remorse.

Sell Stuff for Savings

Most of us have loads of "stuff" that we have bought and hardly use. Instead of these items gathering dust, consider what they are worth new and set a price where you can sell it online. This is an excellent way to get out of debt or bump up your emergency savings.

These items can be advertised online, via Facebook community pages, or even local community pages or advertisements in shopping centers. Commit to clearing out anything and everything that you have not used within the last six to twelve months, and advertise each item for sale.

You may be pleasantly surprised by just how much you are able to collect to add toward your emergency saving account immediately.

Stay Personally Informed of Trends

Educate yourself regarding what is happening in the world of finance. When new tax directives are passed into law, be sure that you understand them and the financial implications that they will have on you in the future. This is your life and your finances.

You need to assume responsibility and accept accountability for the direction your life takes and being able to support yourself financially. Become financially astute by reading blogs and financial articles. Speak to a financial adviser if there is something you do not understand. They are usually more than happy to share their expertise with someone who is genuinely interested in taking their finances seriously.

Try an Ad-Blocker

We mentioned earlier that your browsing history usually determines which advertisements appear during searches (often tempting you to spend money that you do not have). You can easily avoid all of these advertisements by turning on an ad-blocking app. Once you have done so, you can quickly see how these adverts accumulate and take control of your life online.

Even social media outlets like Facebook and YouTube have so many advertisements that you cannot scroll for a few minutes without having something trying to distract you. This is where search engine optimization comes into play. Each of these sites generally know more about the personal preferences that you have on a subconscious level than you are even aware of yourself. Installing an ad-blocker will not get rid of every single advertisement, but it will certainly go a long way in minimizing them.

Wi-Fi

If you are on a contract with your cell phone, do your best to connect with your home and work Wi-Fi as soon as you arrive at either destination. This will save you from running over your data cap on your cell phone contract and facing huge charges. You can save on all of these by making use of your uncapped fixed Wi-Fi connection.

Good Money Habits

A sure way to get your finances under control is to adopt some sound financial habits. Here are some of our top tips when it comes to keeping your finances looking healthy:

Avoid Late Payments

Be sure that you know what you owe to whom at every given moment and what your current financial situation looks like. If you have a banking app on your cell phone, this is simple enough to set up and ensure that you are notified the moment there is any movement on your account(s).

Some people may think it is an inconvenience to have their phone going off all the time, but it is also an early warning system to report fraud if someone has either cloned your card or you are the victim of identity theft. In this case, you should contact your financial institution immediately and have your card(s) canceled and reissued as a matter of urgency.

Budget According to Life Goals

Figure out what you really want out of life, and budget according to these goals versus actual numbers. Earlier we used the example of a family vacation as a goal. You can only reach this goal, however, if you have all your financial information at your disposal.

Connect your life goals to your financial goals by making them more realistic concerning what you want out of life. You may want a new car, a new home, or to make a down payment to open your very own business. Just seeing a figure is seldom going to ensure that your goal is achieved.

Check How You Are Doing Regularly

You fought so hard to get out of debt, so it is important to take your financial temperature on a regular basis. Just as you would take a trip to your friendly general practitioner to have a health check-up every few months, check on your financial health regularly. You can do this by reviewing your free credit reports as they become available; you could even set reminders for when each is available.

The main reason for checking this information is to be sure that nothing has changed. If you come across any discrepancies, follow the procedure that we have already mentioned to submit a query in writing to the bureau. Understand that they have some time to investigate the discrepancy. It does not help to be impatient about receiving this information.

If you notice that you have payments that have been listed as short-paid or even skipped, investigate these, and if you are at fault, make a plan urgently to catch up on any and all outstanding payments.

Conduct these checks on a regular basis to be sure that your credit score is still healthy.

Delayed Gratification

Practice self-control when it comes to wanting something in particular. This means setting aside enough funds to be able to pay cash for what you want. This will often remove the instant gratification syndrome that many of us suffer from when we are deep in debt. This will be replaced with delayed gratification instead—except this will not include the guilt and anxiety felt after having overspent on something.

By saving for whatever it is that you want, you can avoid experiencing all those panicked feelings due to not knowing whether you can actually afford your expense or not.

Hustle Permanently

Side hustles are definitely a lucrative way of making additional money. Depending on what you are doing and what the average return is on your time, you may discover that the side hustle is paying you more than your current wages are. This will require some serious thought and consideration.

If you are receiving bonuses, have a 401k, or receive other allowances, then you may be sacrificing a sure thing for something that is not necessarily guaranteed. If, however, you are currently operating in a field where your employment is not guaranteed and you can easily replace your current income by working a little harder at your side hustle, then it may be time for you to do it permanently.

Nobody can decide this for you. It takes some serious consideration and weighing of all the options before diving in feet-first.

Only Use Credit You Can Repay

Remember to use credit sparingly in order to maintain your current credit score. Do not overspend using your credit cards. The best piece of advice to follow would be to only spend the amount of credit that you know you will be able to repay at the end of the month.

Save Monthly

Make monthly saving a top priority. You should at least be adding to your emergency fund. If you have a family, consider opening a college fund for your children, and you also may want to think about setting aside funds toward your retirement.

This seems to be an awful lot of savings, but once you are out of debt, you will see that funds you would have been allocating toward paying off debt can quite easily be split into these three categories and you can still live quite comfortably.

Shop Savings, Specials, and Seasons

Remember to shop for savings, specials, and seasons. Scratch through bargain bins for specials that you know will be hard to beat. You can often pick up clothing at extra-low bargain prices that are end-of-range or out of season. When it comes to buying foods, look for items that are marked down but still within the expiration date. Fresh fruits and vegetables within season are usually cheaper than crops that are imported and not in season.

Spend Less Than Your Budget

You can tap into frugal living by making a decision to try to live on less than you budget each month. This can be difficult to achieve at first, but it is not impossible. It will involve careful planning, being wiser with your money, and still having money left over at the end of each month. Anything less could lead to sliding back into debt.

Conclusion

"Most of the important things in the world have been accomplished by people who have kept on trying when there seemed to be no hope at all." ~ *Dale Carnegie*

Debt-Free Living

So, you are finally out of the debt pit and plan to stay out. But what does a debt-free life look like? Does this mean that you continue to live a life of total frugality forevermore? What are the major differences between those who are still living large on their credit cards from month to month versus what your new life will be?

To answer your questions, you are not going to be bothered by debt collection agencies anymore or receive calls from the credit card company (other than to possibly offer you credit again). That in itself should bring you a whole lot of peace and joy. The knot in the pit of your stomach that develops each time the phone rings should also begin to slowly untangle itself.

You are now part of only a select group of people—ones who have consciously chosen to climb out of that pit no matter what it took. You can congratulate yourself and be really proud that you never gave up halfway, throwing the towel in. You toughened up, tightened your belt as much as possible, and hunkered down for the long haul. However long it took you to claw your way out, you are now finally free. You have joined part of only 20% of American households that can make the claim that they are free from the chains of debt that will continue to keep them in bondage until they decide to do something about it.

According to the reputable credit bureau Experian, in 2019, the average American had debt to the tune of $90,460. In their report, they even went so far as to break these figures down by age group, and what was not surprising is that Gen X, or those falling in the 40 to 55 age group, are sitting with an average debt of $135,841. The least debt is carried by Gen Z (18- to 23-year-olds), who are indebted with an average of $9,593. Dave Ramsey confirms that 8 out of 10 people have so much debt that it is negatively influencing every area of their lives. He explains, "It backs you into a corner and stands between you and your dreams. Debt drains your hope" (Ramsey, n.d.).

Settling to be one of these statistics is where hopelessness creeps in, and this does not need to be the case. Change is possible, but it all begins with a willingness to be prepared to follow through. The tenacity and sheer guts and determination are the only things that can see you actually making a plan to construct a ladder strong enough to get you out of the debt pit—but, it is possible.

What will the end result look like? What will it feel like on the day that you make that final payment on your mortgage, your car, or your student loan? How wonderful will it be knowing that the next day, you can wake up full of hope? Where millions of Americans refuse to make these changes, you decided to hang in there and see it through. Why? Because you could visualize what tomorrow would look like.

This group includes select individuals and families who decided that debt is not welcome in their homes. This group of people manages to survive on less than what they earn month after month. They have a decent amount of money in their emergency fund and are actively saving for other worthwhile goals. What makes these people different is they were prepared to do whatever it took to get to this point. They recognized that they were drowning in debt, but when that life-raft was thrown their way, they immediately recognized it for what it was and hung on for dear life.

There are actually a number of characteristics that most of these individuals share, which are detailed below.

They Are Comfortable Saying No

For individuals who have worked through their debt crisis and come out the other end smelling like roses, they know what saying no feels like, and they are quite comfortable uttering this word. They are not easy to convince when it comes to taking on further debt. If anything, they are adamant about staying as far away from any form of debt. They know how hard they had to work to get to this point.

They Are Giving

Living a life free of debt comes from being kind, giving, and compassionate toward others. It is being able to recognize when someone has a need that is greater than yours and being prepared to answer the call immediately. They have more because they are willing to give more. It is not always just money or materialistic things that they are willing to give. In many instances, they will offer their time and their talents to those they come across who are in need. Because they need less themselves, it becomes easier to recognize when others are reaching out.

They will volunteer, donate, visit, and generally be kind with all the gifts that they have. Living a life with less while getting out of debt has taught them to appreciate the little things more.

They Are Not Materialistic

Before they started this journey to becoming totally debt-free, most of these people will admit that it was all about the stuff they had. They had to have the nicest house or the most expensive car, or their children needed to attend the finest school and participate in every possible activity. Days were kept so full of things to do, yet they were empty. They lacked true meaning.

Now, they will tell you that none of those things matter. They have simplified their lives. Their expensive car might have been sold for something more reasonable so they were able to pay cash for it, or perhaps they decided to move to a more affordable neighborhood.

Right at the beginning of this book, we discussed selling some of the items that you own that are hardly ever used as a means of saving $1,000. By the end of that process, you should have already started feeling somewhat lighter. When we are surrounded by all sorts of belongings, they demand to either be used, maintained, or cleaned. What makes this offloading process so cathartic is that you can really get rid of some of the clutter that makes you feel claustrophobic after a while.

This is also a way to be able to save money and free up some of your debts. This puts into perspective exactly what some of these items are worth and how much money you have potentially thrown away trying to keep up with the Joneses.

When all is said and done, you are not what you own. Once you realize this, you can truly begin to make changes to your lifestyle. Living frugally may have been one of the ways that you have managed to get to this point. Frugality teaches you not only how to manage your money better, but it teaches you to have a greater appreciation for all the things you already have. Quite honestly, when do you get to the point of being able to say that enough is enough when it comes to how much stuff you actually own?

They Are Passionate

Getting out of debt and staying that way has become a passionate lifestyle that has called for many tough choices. Because they have had a laser-like focus on sorting out their debts, they could chip away at them one dollar at a time. They were aware of their end goal and could see where they wanted to be (debt-free). It did not matter to them that they were going to have to work hard to get to this point; they simply continued to push through until the very end.

They Are Prepared to Make Sacrifices

Getting out of debt means having to make a great deal of sacrifices, so you must be prepared to do so no matter the cost. These sacrifices may have included a complete lifestyle change, such as giving up friends who were not prepared to support these changes.

Luxury items would have definitely set aside, as well as entertainment and family vacations. Becoming debt-free can never be a one-sided commitment from one member of the family single-handedly attempting to do so. It requires participation from every member of the family.

Making small, incremental sacrifices by giving up things that were thought to be important should be easier]over time. It should become easier to give up cable TV and other forms of entertainment when quality family time is had instead.

For those who have gotten out of debt, no sacrifice was too great. This is not to say that it was quick or easy. Anyone looking for a shortcut will soon be disappointed. However, the benefits of seeing it through to the end will certainly be worth the advantages.

They Are Self-Disciplined

Budgeting for things monthly and living within and below your actual budget may have demanded the very last ounce of self-discipline that you were able to muster. There may have even been times when you felt like giving up and returning to your previous "comfortable" lifestyle. But then you are suddenly reminded of everything that accompanied that package deal—the stress, the anxiety, and even depression because you did not have a proper handle on your financial situation.

Self-discipline meant that you were prepared to skip your morning latte at Starbucks, settling for conventional coffee at home instead. It meant brown-bagging lunches for work and school versus ordering something from the local deli. It also meant sacrificing ordering take-out, visiting the drive-through, and even giving up date nights for a while. It meant that you were prepared to do whatever it took to get to where you currently are.

They Disrupt the Status Quo

Settling your debt should be more important than listening to whatever everyone else is doing. It means not buying into the myth that there is no way for you to survive unless you carry multiple credit cards, your home is refinanced, or you have a revolving credit plan in place, as well as outstanding student loans. This is not the way you should live; however, it is the way that banks and all the lending companies want you to live.

The great news is that you chose not to go that route. Instead, you chose to swim upstream against the current. Yes, it might have taken you a lot longer than you would have liked, but the truth is, you are now out of it completely, and you never have to look over your shoulder ever again.

They Do Not Compete

The whole "keeping up with the Joneses" routine has become old and jaded. The blindfold was removed a while back, and you realized that when it came to personal finance, you were probably living from paycheck to paycheck and maxing out their credit cards just to look the part. The truth is that the "lifestyle" that is being projected is just one big lie, and you managed to see through it in time.

You now hold yourself responsible and accountable, without all the pressure of having to keep up appearances with anyone (which is exhausting). You are currently more than satisfied with what you have, because you can finally say that everything you possess is bought, paid for, and owned by you. It may have taken you three to five years to get to this point, and it might have been a rough couple of years. However, looking back at the lessons you learned, you should not want to change a thing.

They Know What They Want

Goals are what has driven them to get to this point of financial freedom—that and actively working toward each goal's achievement each and every day. Some goals were way bigger than others, but they learned to break each of these down into smaller, more manageable ones that were achievable. They celebrated their wins and got back up each time they fell down rather than staying down and admitting defeat. Thanks to goal-setting they were able to drive down each of their debts to get to the point where they finally were able to manage to make final payments on every debt that was due.

They now know what it feels like to go without, to live a frugal life, to save each month, and to make better, wiser purchasing decisions. For them, this has become a way of life rather than just a means of settling their debts. They realize that they can still enjoy some of the luxuries of enjoying a coffee once in a while or going out to a movie or dinner, so long as each of these were carefully planned and budgeted ahead of time, rather than slipping back into old habits because they are now debt-free.

How to Live a Debt-Free Life

Most people find that it is impossible to live without some form of credit. The good news is that there are a lot of people (especially the older generation) who figured out years ago that this was not the smartest way to go. Many of these individuals do not even have bank accounts. They operate strictly on a cash basis. If they do not have the cash, the purchase is not made.

Buy Your Home with Cash

Most individuals will say that it is downright impossible to save up in order to pay for a home without financial assistance from somewhere. Try to consider a couple of options that may actually work in your favor and allow you to purchase your home with cash. The first is to find a home that is listed as a "rent to own" property. In this case, you are paying toward the mortgage already on someone else's property with the intention of owning the property yourself.

Look for a place that is cheaper than what you are prepared to spend each month. Invest the balance of what you would have paid into a high-yield-savings account. With this type of investment account, you cannot withdraw your investment for a specified term that you can choose yourself.

As you continue to pay into this account, you will see your investment grow at an exponential rate. These accounts offer up to 20 times more than a normal savings account. Only once you know you have enough cash saved up should you make an offer on the property. An additional benefit of transacting this way is that you get to save on all the compounding interest that would normally form part of purchasing the property. You are likely to get away with property taxes as well as all the interest.

For those who are still skeptical, understand that it can and has been done; the secret is shopping around for a place that you can afford. Another important thing is finding a cheap enough property that you can afford to still set aside a decent amount of cash each month.

Buying Power of Cash

There is certainly buying power when it comes to making cash purchases. You have the upper hand in being able to negotiate with sellers, because they are often keener to be paid in cash than having to fund some of the credit card transactions and service fees themselves. Look at high-value items at bargain prices that you know you can afford, and then begin the negotiation process.

One item that you should consider paying cash for include cars. While a brand new car is extremely appealing, it depreciates considerably over a four-year payment term (if you had to buy it on credit), let alone all the interest that you happen to be paying along with your normal monthly payment.

For any credit payment, whether it is credit cards, revolving personal loans, or student loans, there is always interest attached. Depending on your credit score, this rate of interest will either be higher than normal or slightly lower. However, interest is interest, and it is the equivalent of throwing money away.

This is the reason why you should do your best to save for everything that you want until you have enough money to make the purchase you desire.

Consider Online Payment Options

There are various online payment options available that don't require credit or debit cards. Consider looking into PayPal and other financial transaction services that are prepared to work with cash. The transaction fees are often much lower than what banks and other financial institutions are prepared to offer you.

Get That Emergency Fund Saved

The secret to staying out of debt is ensuring that you have your emergency fund saved. Once you are completely financially independent, you will be able to increase your investment toward this fund. Or, you can divide the funds you have at your disposal toward other investments, whether you are planning to invest in your retirement or setting up college funds for your children's futures.

If you manage to start this when your children are still young, by the time that this money is needed, there should be a nice sum available, so you will not need to get sucked into one of the biggest money pits eating away at the American economy at the moment—student loans. Believe me, your children will thank you for it.

Rent Cash

This is often a hotly debated topic. Many people would recommend owning versus renting, yet there are specific benefits to renting your home before you decide to settle down. Firstly, while renting, you can get a feel for the house with all of its flaws (which are often not discussed when viewing a property to purchase). So long as you are renting, should something go wrong, it becomes your landlord's problem rather than yours.

You can get to know the neighborhood better, as well, such as the schools, shops, and infrastructure that is in the immediate area. This will either confirm that the property is right for you or give you the option of finding another property that is better suited to your specific needs.

While this definitely has a whole lot of benefits attached to it, it can also turn into a nightmare when your landlord refuses to take any responsibility for things that go wrong with the house.

As a tenant, you have certain rights that you can take up with relevant authorities. Your rights are protected as long as you are doing your part, such as making your payments on a monthly basis and keeping the property in the same condition you received it in. In fact, as a tenant, it is always better to leave any property in a better condition than it was when you moved in.

Replace Your Credit Card(s)

We have briefly discussed getting rid of all of your credit cards and opting for either a standard checking account or a debit card. Many individuals will argue that you cannot process most transactions using a debit card. I'm here to burst that bubble completely. A debit card operates exactly the same way as a credit card, with the exception that you are not paying interest on any outstanding amounts. This is because unless you have a positive balance in your account, it will not allow you to transact. Thus, unless you have cash in your account, transactions will simply be declined.

The beauty of this is that you have full control over your finances, preventing them from running away from you. So, it is true that anything you are able to do with a credit card can be done using a debit card (besides running up debt). It is definitely a much safer option than simply swiping today and worrying about how you are going to pay your debt off later.

Save for What You Want

Let's say you have seen a stunning couch set that you know will look just perfect in your living area. The price tag is reasonable. Before you rush out and open a store account, divide the cost of the cash price of the account by the amount of money you know you can comfortably set aside toward this item. It may take you a couple of months to be able to save the amount of money you would ideally like to spend on this furniture.

As soon as you have enough money saved, it is time to start negotiating with the store owner for a better price for cash. Guess what? Sometimes, you may actually get a few hundred dollars knocked off the price. This is certainly a better option than paying more than double the amount to the store in interest alone because you have decided to purchase it with credit.

Next to most advertisements, they will have both a cash price and a credit price. Notice the difference between the two? By now, you should be smiling broadly. Aren't you pleased that you finally took the time to figure out your finances and work your way out of the debt trap?

Travel with Cash

Another myth that we are going to debunk is the fact that you cannot travel without a credit card. Most people would have you believe that you cannot get a room in a hotel, book an airplane ticket, or reserve a car unless you have a credit card. This is not true. Most of these vendors are more than happy to deal with cash. You may even be rewarded with an upgrade or additional discount because you are paying this way.

Some further secrets when it comes to travel are to look at booking your tickets as far in advance as possible and shopping around for the best prices. Whether it is a red-eye flight or you get a substantial discount because you've made your booking months in advance, take advantage of each of these discounted options.

Maintain a Debt-Free Lifestyle

Despite what the masses out there have to say, it is possible for you to maintain a lifestyle that is free of debt. This is great news, especially if it has taken you several years to get to this point. Some examples of this are compulsive savers who settle on a particular amount of money that they allow themselves to spend during a specific time. This would cover all of their basic necessities as well as any other wants.

If you happen to have been buying specials and building on your food supplies slowly and steadily, there may even come a time when you can spend money on only the bare essentials for the month and pump your monthly grocery budget into savings.

Consider Community Colleges

If you happen to be thinking about furthering your education, consider community colleges as possible options rather than picking up the difference at private universities or colleges. The cost savings when considering these two options alongside one another is huge.

According to the National Society of High School Scholars, the average community college runs at an annual cost of around $3,500, while universities can cost up to $35,000 per year for a student who is attending a school outside of their home state.

Credit Card Payments

You may still have a credit card that you are holding on to just to keep a particular credit score. If this is the route that you have chosen to take with your finances, be sure to pay off all your debts for the month. Pay your accounts in full either before or on the due date every single month to avoid sliding back into a situation where you are faced with debt.

Be certain that you only make small purchases on the card, and set the money aside immediately to settle your credit card debt the moment it is due to be paid. Remember to use your card sparingly and only as a means of keeping your credit score.

Spend Only as Necessary

We are often tempted to spend all of our allocated budget each month, whether there's some additional money left over or not. By paying close attention to your budget and only purchasing those items that are necessary and on your list, you can actually save money.

It can be tempting to add items to your shopping cart that are not on your list and that are minor luxuries, but this is not advisable. Getting into the habit of putting a detailed list together and then sticking to this list will restore the power you have over your finances. You may just be surprised at just how far your budget will stretch (even including the odd luxury item).

The most important thing is to shop according to your list, purchasing no more and no less. If it's not on the list, leave it on the shelf in the store.

What a Debt-Free Lifestyle Really Looks Like

When you are living in debt, you are existing under a constant cloud of chaos and uncertainty. Living with debt leads to stressful situations, often resulting in divorce because couples are constantly fighting about money problems. It is easy to understand how debt can add strain on a relationship. This is why getting out of debt and living a debt-free lifestyle is so important.

Below are some of the reasons for striving to live debt-free. These benefits include things like better relationships and improved health. Those who have fought their way out from under a pile of debt definitely deserve to live this kind of lifestyle.

Balance Between Life and Work

Your work-life balance is finally able to improve because you no longer need to hold down two or three jobs to get out of debt. Once you are out of the hole, it becomes possible for you to go back to one regular job. This means being able to evenly balance your work and home life once more without having to sacrifice one for the other.

Credit Score

Your credit score will improve over time. If you can get your creditors to actually remove any and all late payment or default information, or if they make notes that certain debts have been repaid, your score will slowly begin to improve. This is especially true when you do not close out your accounts.

Look at keeping one credit card open with a really low credit limit. Use this card sparingly each month, and be sure to pay the full amount.

Fall-Back Plan

You are free to live your life with less risk than the average individual because you have been building up your emergency fund and continue to do so. Right now, your balance is looking rather healthy, and you can allocate part of this toward setting up your own side hustle or even running the small, calculated risk of possibly opening your own business.

The reason for this is that you are not having to loan any money from any source other than yourself. It should be mentioned that you should only do this if your emergency fund is way over your required budget, and you know that should something go wrong, you are prepared to sacrifice this amount of money.

Give More Freely

Because you now do not have that millstone of debt hanging around your neck anymore, you can recognize the need in others and be prepared to help out. It always seems that those who have the most to give and who are prepared to do so more freely have this and more come back to them.

Greater Disposable Income

This benefit seems to be an obvious one. If you are now debt-free, by rights you no longer owe anyone anything. This will result in having more disposable income available to you at the end of each month. It needs to be stated here that this does not mean that you should go on a shopping spree to ensure that you get rid of every last dime. There are far more beneficial things you can do with this income, which are touched upon as you keep reading.

Health

Your overall health will improve because you are no longer worrying about what is happening with your finances. Because your health is improved, your medical bills will be driven down proportionately. You will need fewer medical visits, and you will begin to feel better about yourself. You will also be driven to make lifestyle changes to support healthy living so you can lead a happier life that is more fulfilling than it was before.

Improved Employment

Having a better credit score assists you in finding better employment, especially since more and more organizations are pushing through credit checks as part of their hiring protocols.

Instead of avoiding each listed job because it indicated that your credit score needed to be healthy, you can now look forward to being able to apply for any opening with confidence. You no longer need to be embarrassed or ashamed about your credit rating.

Perhaps you can apply somewhere that you were too afraid to apply before because you were afraid someone might discover the truth about your financial situation. But that was then, and this is now. You can deal with any credit checks with confidence.

Improved Relationships

Since you have managed to get out of the debt pit, your relationships with your spouse and those around you have improved. You appear to be happier and less stressed out, because you no longer have to worry about your current financial situation. You are able to discuss things more openly without conversations escalating into arguments because life is so tough or unbearable. For the first time in a long time, you are able to look toward the future with hope and a cheerful attitude.

Investments

Because you have all this additional disposable income, you can now begin investing money wisely so it can grow as exponentially as possible. You may have a goal where you would like to retire sooner than you had originally planned. Your goals have now also shifted from focusing on getting out of debt to saving and doing more with the current money that you do have.

Once you are ready to begin investing, please do yourself a favor and work with a financial advisor as they will be more financially astute than you are. They will be able to advise you as to where you can find the best place(s) to invest your capital for maximum growth.

Live Life Better

You will have the opportunity to live your life better than you would have been able to do if you were still saddled with all that debt. The reason for this is that you will be free from the stress and anxiety you experienced when you had debt collection agencies or creditors calling you almost daily to deal with accounts that are past-due.

You will have more disposable income on hand to be able to save for whatever it is that you really want, whether this is your dream family holiday or a new major appliance for your home. You will now be aware that making some short-term sacrifices are well worth the long-term benefits of not owing anyone anything.

Mental Health Benefits

For once in your life, you can breathe easier, you manage to sleep better, and you no longer battle with fits of anxiety or depression. You have truly been able to find the answer to being happier. You start to notice your general health improving, resulting in fewer doctor's visits.

If you are on chronic medication for any stress-related problems, the chances are that one of the underlying causes was actually linked to your financial problems. Once these problems have been resolved, in conjunction with your doctor and/or specialist, you may be able to cut back on some of your medication, which will benefit your finances even more. This is especially true if your medical insurance only covers a portion of your medications.

Retire Sooner

You may have always dreamed of being able to retire earlier in order to travel the world and do all those things that you would really like to do while you are still young enough to enjoy it. Once you are out of your financial troubles and able to live completely debt-free, this may be something that you can add to your bucket list and begin saving toward seriously. This is usually only a good idea if you have some form of passive income that is still coming in that can at least allow you to live comfortably.

Your next steps would be to figure out how much this dream of yours is going to cost, save that amount of cash by following the patterns and processes we have outlined in this book, set yourself some financial goals and milestones that you know you can achieve, and then actively work toward achieving them.

Retirement is a big deal, and you need to be certain that you have enough funds in the bank, invested, or saved to be able to live comfortably until you die. Otherwise, you need to have a back-up plan or hobby that you know will be able to pay out the amount of money you need to survive and thrive monthly.

Self-Esteem

An area that always takes a huge toll when we are in a financial slump is our self-esteem. We constantly feel like we are a failure; we have failed ourselves, our lifelong partners, and our family.

It is comforting to know that this can all be turned around once you are debt-free. You will be able to hold your head up high wherever you go. Remember that only two out of every eight Americans can actually do this, because the rest of them are up to their necks in debt and still drowning.

Remember that nervous feeling that you would get whenever someone mentioned money, accounts, finance, or debt? You no longer have to feel that way, because you have fought long and hard to restore your name; you've battled through some dark times to finally be able to make that last payment. You have something to really be extremely proud of, so do not let anyone ever steal that feeling from you or make you feel like you have not earned it.

Marriage and Time for Parenting

One of the final benefits of living debt-free is by no means a small one. Your marital relationship and your role as a parent will also change for the better. During the tough times of digging your way out of debt, you would have had to stand by each other.

Together, you made some major sacrifices, and it may have taken you years to get to the place where you are now. Do not forget all the good times and the magical memories that you were able to make together as a family unit while surviving the tough times. If you have learned anything through this process, it should be that your spouse or life partner and your children should come first in your life—always.

Before you got to this point, you may have thought that it was all about whatever materialistic things you could accumulate. Most likely, taking the time to be together as a family was not high on your list of priorities because it was all about the "stuff" you were gathering.

You have finally been able to put your life into perspective and see that everything is exactly the opposite. It has nothing to do with materialism, but rather it has to do with relationships. You have had the unique opportunity of being able to strengthen these relationships by doing simple things together. The simple things somehow turned out to be the best decisions over the last few years. The end result has been that you are now striving to be the best spouse or partner that you can be, as well as the best possible parent, hoping to leave a legacy that your children can adopt and follow.

The greatest gift that you could ever leave your children is teaching them how to deal with money wisely so that they never have to be in debt themselves. Teach your children how to budget and the value of saving for things that they want, rather than being drawn to instant gratification. There is a much better way to work with money, and discovering this for themselves will create a new generation of young people who are wiser about working with money.

The main point of the lessons, steps, and processes outlined in this book is to help you become financially independent, no matter how long it takes. There is hope in store, even when your financial situation looks as bleak as can be. By following the steps we have outlined and by being tenaciously focused on regaining control over your life, you too can experience for yourself freedom from the bondage that comes with debt. Do not give in to temptations that will certainly be thrown in your direction. Be prepared for this to be a lengthy process initially and then a lifelong lifestyle. Change is never easy, but it is always worth it!

Now that you have all of the tools you need to climb out of the debt pit, what are you waiting for? It is time to make some major changes in your life and your lifestyle. All you need to do is take the first step, which is making the decision that you are tired of being broke all the time, and you really want to be financially free. The next step will require being ready to do whatever it takes to make slow and steady progress.

So, settle in, and watch your debt decrease more and more as you make whatever sacrifices may be necessary.

As an author, I welcome and rely on my readers' feedback. If you have enjoyed this book and found value in its pages, please do me the honor of leaving a review online. I wish you the best of luck on your journey toward a debt-free life!

References

Bacon, N. (2014, November 5). *How to create a budget: A 6-step guide*. Natalie Bacon. https://www.nataliebacon.com/how-to-create-budget/

Beck, J. (2018a, April 23). *How one 29-year-old paid off $43K in the San Francisco Bay area*. JackieBeck.com. https://www.jackiebeck.com/how-one-29-year-old-paid-off-43k-bay-area/

Beck, J. (2018b, July 12). *The secret to staying motivated when getting out of debt*. JackieBeck.com. https://www.jackiebeck.com/the-secret-to-staying-motivated-when-getting-out-of-debt/

Beck, J. (2019, April 17). *6 Get out of debt stories that will amaze & inspire you*. JackieBeck.com. https://www.jackiebeck.com/get-out-of-debt-stories/

Bell, G. (2014, May 12). *Where did personal responsibility go?* Debt RoundUp. https://www.debtroundup.com/personal-responsibility-is-dead/

Best Debt Companys. (n.d.). *Top 25 reasons people go into debt*. BestDebtCompanys.com.

https://bestdebtcompanys.com/top-25-reasons-people-go-into-debt/

Boitnott, J. (2019, December 19). *10 Reasons people go into debt*. Debt.com. https://www.debt.com/news/how-do-people-get-into-debt/

BrainyQuote. (n.d.-a). *936 Debt quotes - Inspirational quotes at BrainyQuote*. BrainyQuote. https://www.brainyquote.com/topics/debt-quotes

BrainyQuote. (n.d.-b). *Leo Burnett quotes*. BrainyQuote. Retrieved November 8, 2020, from https://www.brainyquote.com/quotes/leo_burnett_103239?src=t_reach_for_the_stars

Bresino, T. (2010, October 19). *What's the No. 1 reason people go into debt?* HowStuffWorks. https://money.howstuffworks.com/personal-finance/debt-management/reason-people-go-into-debt.htm

Caldwell, M. (2019, February 2). *4 Steps to help you stop going into debt each month*. The Balance. https://www.thebalance.com/how-to-stop-going-into-debt-each-month-2385988

Credit Counselling Society. (n.d.-a). *12 Fastest and most effective ways to get out of debt*. Credit Counselling Society. https://www.nomoredebts.org/blog/money/management/12-ways-to-get-out-of-debt

Credit Counselling Society. (n.d.-b). *How to deal & communicate with creditors & collection agencies & pay off debt.* Www.Nomoredebts.org. https://www.nomoredebts.org/debt-help/dealing-with-creditors/communicating-with-creditors-and-collection-agencies

Dr., J. (2018, February 16). *How this doctor is paying off $1.9 million in debt.* JackieBeck.com. https://www.jackiebeck.com/doctor-paying-off-debt/

Dulin, J. (2019, April 17). *11 Best ways to stay motivated when paying off debt.* MoneySmartGuides.com. https://www.moneysmartguides.com/how-to-stay-motivated-when-paying-off-debt

Fay, B. (2018, February 15). *10 Mistakes people make when trying to get out of debt.* Debt.org. https://www.debt.org/blog/10-mistakes-getting-out-of-debt/

Fesenmyer Cousino Weinzimmer Attorneys. (2018, May 24). *Are you in debt? You're not alone.* FCW. https://www.fcwlegal.com/are-you-in-debt-youre-not-alone/

Gobler, E. (2019, February 18). *21 Goals to set for yourself to make 2020 your best year ever.* Erin Gobler. https://eringobler.com/goals-to-set/

Hecht, A. (2019, December 19). *How to stop obsessing over your debt, according to experts.* CNBC; CNBC. https://www.cnbc.com/2019/12/19/how-to-stop-obsessing-over-your-debt-according-to-experts.html

Hill, A. (2017, December 28). *How we paid off our $195,000 mortgage in 4 years.* JackieBeck.com. https://www.jackiebeck.com/paid-off-our-195000-mortgage-in-4-years/

Johnson, H. (2018, November). *11 Ways to get out of debt faster.* The Simple Dollar; TheSimpleDollar.com. https://www.thesimpledollar.com/credit/manage-debt/11-ways-to-get-out-of-debt-faster/

Kumok, Z. (2014, November 10). *What it takes to be debt free when you make $30,000 a year.* JackieBeck.com. https://www.jackiebeck.com/what-it-takes-to-be-debt-free-on-30k-a-year/

Liv. (2017, February 9). *19 Ways to stay motivated while paying off debt.* Funding Cloud Nine. https://www.fundingcloudnine.com/stay-motivated-paying-off-debt/

Livingston, A. (2020, November 5). *How to deal with creditors & bill collection agencies and protect yourself.* Moneycrashers.com. https://www.moneycrashers.com/how-to-deal-with-creditors-and-collection-agencies/

Mantilla, S. (2020, April 22). *Budgeting tips for beginners: How to start a budget that works.* Money Tamer. https://moneytamer.com/budgeting-tips-for-beginners/

May, P. (2008, September 12). *50 years later, how the credit card has changed America.* The Mercury News. https://www.mercurynews.com/2008/09/12/50-years-later-how-the-credit-card-has-changed-america/

Mayberry, M. (2017, January 18). *10 Great quotes on the power of goals.* Entrepreneur. https://www.entrepreneur.com/article/287411

NerdWallet Blog. (n.d.). *How they ditched debt.* NerdWallet. https://www.nerdwallet.com/blog/finance/getting-out-of-debt-stories/

Nicole. (2017, April 14). *Got debt? If you are in a hole, stop digging!* Frugal Chic Life. https://www.frugalchiclife.com/got-debt-hole-stop-digging/

Peach, C. (2015, November 2). *What it took for this couple to pay off debt fast.* JackieBeck.com. https://www.jackiebeck.com/we-were-tired-of-being-broke/

Peiffer, E. (2019, December 19). *Debt in America: An interactive map.* Urbn.Is. https://apps.urban.org/features/debt-interactive-map/

Pleasant, L. (2014, May 22). *Our economy wants you to be in debt - Five things you can do to take charge.* Yes Magazine. https://www.yesmagazine.org/economy/2014/

05/22/our-economy-wants-you-to-be-in-debt-five-things-you-can-do-to-take-charge/

Ramsey, D. (n.d.). *25 Ways to get out of debt*. Daveramsey.com. https://www.daveramsey.com/blog/ways-to-get-out-of-debt

Ramsey, D. (2018). *10 Reasons people stay in debt*. Daveramsey.com. https://www.daveramsey.com/blog/why-do-people-stay-in-debt

Smart Dollar. (n.d.). *5 Reasons people stay in debt*. Smartdollar.com. https://www.smartdollar.com/blog/5-reasons-people-stay-in-debt

Swanson, A. (2015, June 16). These powerful photos of people living with debt will make you feel not alone. *Washington Post*. https://www.washingtonpost.com/news/wonk/wp/2015/06/16/these-powerful-photos-of-people-living-with-debt-will-make-you-feel-not-alone/

The Ascent Staff. (2019, May 21). *Study: The psychological cost of debt*. The Motley Fool. https://www.fool.com/the-ascent/research/study-psychological-cost-debt/

Touryalai, H. (2014, February 21). *$1 Trillion student loan problem keeps getting worse*. Forbes. https://www.forbes.com/sites/halahtouryalai/

2014/02/21/1-trillion-student-loan-problem-keeps-getting-worse/

Image References

Images courtesy of Pixabay.com

Images courtesy of Pexels.com

Images courtesy of Unsplash.com

www.ingramcontent.com/pod-product-compliance
Lightning Source LLC
Chambersburg PA
CBHW011404210526
45464CB00010B/3041